Wake Up!

Wake Up!

AWAKENING TO YOUR TRUE SELF

GURPREET

iUniverse LLC
Bloomington

WAKE UP!

iUniverse books may be ordered through booksellers or by contacting:

iUniverse
1663 Liberty Drive
Bloomington, IN 47403
www.iuniverse.com
1-800-Authors (1-800-288-4677)

Because of the dynamic nature of the Internet, any web addresses or links contained in this book may have changed since publication and may no longer be valid. The views expressed in this work are solely those of the author and do not necessarily reflect the views of the publisher, and the publisher hereby disclaims any responsibility for them.

Any people depicted in stock imagery provided by Thinkstock are models, and such images are being used for illustrative purposes only.

Certain stock imagery © Thinkstock

ISBN: 978-1-4759-9790-3 (sc)
ISBN: 978-1-4759-9791-0 (e)

Library of Congress Control Number: 2013912471

Printed in the United States of America.

iUniverse rev. date: 07/31/2013

This Is How

Questioner: I understand in my head, but not in my heart. I wonder how?

- Stay with the how you don't understand; this is how.
- When you settle into that little bit that your heart knows, this is how.
- As your hands rest in your heart, this is how.
- When you don't believe in big, this is how.
- When your heart aches, this is how.
- When you are in fire-full longing and your heart melts, this is how.
- When you wish that this longing would never end, this is how.
- When you close all worldly doors and keep your heart open, this is how.
- You only live for this; this is how.
- You only die for this; this is how.
- And love dying in this awakening; this is how.

Contents

About Gurpreet

Gurpreet was born March 22, 1962, and raised in a small village in the Punjab state of India. She has three sisters and a loving mother and father. Her childhood was very carefree and happy, and her family life was filled with love. Growing up she was shy, quiet, and liked to spend time alone. As a child, she had one very close friend, not a big circle of friends. But even so, at school she was loved by the students and the teachers. She once said that, looking back at her schooling and even at college, she realized she spent most of her time in her own world.

At nineteen years of age, in 1981, Gurpreet married. She and her husband immigrated to Edmonton, Alberta, Canada, in 1984. Gurpreet found living in this strange new country very challenging at times, as she had to learn a new language and many new customs. But she eventually adjusted and spent her time fulfilling the demanding roles of a wife and a mother of two sons.

In 1994 the sudden death of a dear cousin shook her deeply, and this caused her to begin her search for answers to the meaning of life. Gurpreet at this time wasn't spiritual and hadn't spent much time thinking about what was beyond everyday life. But the pain of her cousin's death opened her to explore spirituality. Gurpreet explored many different types of meditation, chanting, and mantras, and she read many books and listened to meditation tapes produced by the Osho International Foundation. She began to follow her inner guidance with her whole heart. The very first recognition that came to her was the need to surrender.

Then tragedy struck again. In 1998, at the age of thirty-six, she lost her husband to a heart attack while he was traveling in India with his father. They had been married seventeen years at this time. Gurpreet was in Canada at the time of his death and had to travel to India to cremate her husband.

Gurpreet now had to face the dilemma of how to support her family. As time passed she became an owner of a small hair salon in a nursing home. The pain of her husband's death brought on more longing and fire within Gurpreet, and her search for the truth became even more consuming. While never neglecting her family responsibilities and worldly matters, she devoted herself to her awakening.

Gurpreet stood steadfast and resolute to walk her inner journey. Slowly everyday life started to lose its importance. So earnest was her longing that in 1996 she found a teacher who lived in Edmonton. Being in her teacher's presence, she began to see the created self and her higher self and realized that there was a different way to live. Step-by-step, she kept going deeper and deeper, diminishing in all forms, beliefs, and values, and all of her patterns began to drop. Through this journey she established herself in profound inner purity, knowing, selflessness, and simplicity of heart.

In 2007 she became one with truth; she awakened. This transformational experience led her to enlightenment.

Gurpreet had no desire to be a teacher; her only desire and longing was to keep expanding and to keep going deeper into the awakened state that she was now experiencing. She exuded so much love and warmth that people were profoundly affected by her while in her presence. They were drawn to her and wanted to know more and more about her transformation. Soon a small group of seekers formed and asked Gurpreet if she would teach them how to become awakened. Gurpreet kindly accepted and became an awakened teacher. Gradually the retreats naturally evolved to what they are today. Many people attend these retreats to be with Gurpreet and learn from her teachings. Just being in her presence transforms and awakens us to our higher self.

Gurpreet continues to live in Edmonton and travels internationally and across Canada holding seminars for this true way of being.

A Personal Journey to Gurpreet

Gurpreet's knowledge and insight expressed on these pages is unique and different from anything that has ever been taught before. Her teachings are both simple and profound. As I attended retreats with Gurpreet over the last two years, I began to see that she is truth and have observed many people awaken with her guidance, wisdom and her presence.

The teachings in this book will help the world on their search to self realization. Many seekers are disillusioned and tired of searching for a true teacher, a teacher who will take them to their hearts desire of the awakened state.

I was one of those very exhausted seekers until I met Gurpreet.

My spiritual Journey began when I was fifteen. I was browsing the bookshelves of my community Library when I came across *The Tibetan Book of the Dead*. I was immediately fascinated by the message, that death is not the end; it is simply a transition point in the cycle of many lives. There was something compelling and true on those pages, and it marked the beginning of my very long and difficult search for awakening and self realization.

I spent many years exploring every avenue available to becoming self-realized. As time went by I increasingly began to see that I was no closer to an awakening than when I began. Finally by 2001, after thirty years, I gave up; I ended my search. I concluded that self realization and awakening was for the chosen few and I wasn't among them.

In the autumn of 2011 an email was sent to me saying that a self realized teacher named Gurpreet was coming to the town where I live to conduct a retreat. I hadn't given much thought to attaining self realization for a number of years, so I deleted the email.

A week later I received another email reminding me of this teacher's upcoming visit. This time, rather than deleting it, I paused and reflected; *"What is there to lose."*

So, with a guarded attitude I went to see Gurpreet. The five day retreat with twenty in attendance was my introduction to her. I asked Gurpreet as many questions as I could. Question after question, she didn't bat an eye. She welcomed them all, answering me in a direct yet warm, kind way. There was nothing evasive about her or her answers, something that was immediately attractive.

As the days passed I grew increasingly aware of her presence, she had that "something" that a self realized Master has. But I thought, "What was that to mean for me?" While I wanted the same awareness that she had, I knew from my past experience that the fact that she had it did not mean that I could or would have it also. I needed proof that she was the real thing. Being in her presence would simply not be enough.

Yet I could see that Gurpreet was somehow unique and different. She told us that she had worked for and found her awakening and that she could teach us how to find it too. She told us that being awake is how we are supposed to be, and that we have simply forgotten who we are. By following her walk we can be where she is. Anyone can awaken.

Her message was appealing and refreshing. Her teaching was radical; no spirituality, no dogma, no belief systems, no mysticism. Instead she helps us to see our own belief systems, our patterns and our Ego/Person and to embrace everything we see inside in a warm, kind, and loving way where there is nothing to change and nothing to fix.

What a relief that was. I had spent my life trying to change and fix everything about myself but to no avail. But even though her teachings struck a chord in me that said, "This is Truth," I was still doubtful and I wasn't sure I would go to the next retreat.

Two months went by and as the second retreat approached, something started to stir inside me, a little voice…just go one more time…..I went back and forth in my mind, "No…yes…no…yes." But in the end I went to be with Gurpreet for another five days. This time in her presence I felt a change in me; I felt an unexplained shift. I felt her pure presence and saw how much she shone and poured out love.

In my connection with her I was speechless…her powerful presence and gazing dark eyes pierced my heart. The pain was sharp and for a week after I could feel the ache deep in my chest. I knew then that Gurpreet was the teacher I had been searching for my whole life.

Gurpreet is a rare teacher. She is Truth. Gurpreet is awakening us all to becoming one with our Real Self. It's been this extraordinary journey with nothing to change and nothing to fix and nothing to do but to be and see. To keep the arrow pointed at oneself and embrace everything one sees inside with love, tenderness and softness while basking in Gurpreet's purifying presence.

Carole Davis-McMechan,
Editor

Foreword

In reading and rereading this book, the reader will be grounded deeply in his or her heart by the simplicity and directness of both Gurpreet and her words. Here the reader will find little that may be called complex, sophisticated, or indirect. Gurpreet's words come from a deep, clear, and clean space of knowing within; and with little to be grasped intellectually, her words somehow land directly in the heart, in that space of deep and clear knowing within the reader. Quite simply, Gurpreet engages the reader on the level of the heart, on the level of one's own being, on the level of one's own knowing, and she does it in a way that is as simple as it is real. She is pure beingness relating to another's beingness; thus her frequent responses: "Be kind and gentle with yourself." "Be simple." "Be softened." "Be warmly okay." "Be honest by seeing your dishonesty." "Be in the seeing." "Be in the longing." "Be in it."

Gurpreet's simple and direct teachings center on beingness in the heart. Not the physical heart, of course, but that space within the chest area that we know can tighten, close, and harden as quickly as one's hand can make a clenched fist. We also know, moreover, that the heart naturally loves to let go: to melt swiftly, to open infinitely, and to soften perpetually, often with a light touch of something that may be unintelligible to the mind but is the sweetest nectar to the heart. Without speculating how, but in reference to its effects here, Gurpreet's presence in her words directly touches the heart, again and again, opening and softening it, broadening and deepening that wonderfully clean space within. After soaking up the simple truth infused in this book, the reader will know where the heart is, and there the reader may choose to stay, becoming more and more deeply grounded. As Gurpreet states in her poem, "When you settle into that little bit that your heart knows, this is how."

Most noteworthy is how universal Gurpreet's teachings are. Her responses do not necessarily address how to make one's life better on the outside, but in every single conversation, they always point the reader to something on the inside—to a simple, clean, and true way of being. This is, in part, her great appeal: the underlying message is not one of *doing* anything on the outside or even on the inside but, again, one of beingness in the heart—learning *to see* what is inside of oneself and how *to be* in a true way with anything whatsoever. That said, there may be many reasons readers find this book in their hands: perhaps a feeling that there is something deeper than this life on the surface, but also a lack of knowledge as to how to access it; the pain of discontentment in life; the feeling that life is just not working; a longtime, ardent search for truth; the honoring of one's longing; or mere curiosity. Whatever the reason, no matter the state or condition a person is in, no matter where a person is coming from, one's heart—indeed, one's heart-knowing—can recognize and be deeply touched by Gurpreet's simple, clean, and true way of being.

Finally, in reading this book, the reader may come to realize that by being in Gurpreet's presence with her simple and direct teachings, first here with her words and perhaps later in person, awakening to one's real self and reality is not only possible but inevitable.

Mark Farmer, PhD,
Assistant Professor of Classical Studies, Valparaiso University

Introduction—How to Read This Book

This book incorporates Gurpreet's style of speech, which is an integral part of who she is. Her signature is throughout the book and enhances the powerful essence underlying her message. Gurpreet's language is what makes her so available, so intimate. She is gentle but direct and honest in her words; they touch your heart in a profoundly deep way.

Please note that a glossary is included at the back of the book. It is suggested to peruse this glossary before reading the book to familiarize yourself with Gurpreet's terminology.

This book is divided into two sections. The first section is the open forum, which is a selection of questions and answers from retreats in a group setting held in 2011 and 2012. They have been organized by subject matter.

The second section is composed of transcripts of some of Gurpreet's connections with people. These come from personal time spent with Gurpreet within a group setting. Gurpreet lends her insight to individuals, helping them see and identify their emotions, patterns, and many unseen parts deep inside that make up their created self/ego. These are the things that prevent us from awakening to our real self. The more you are open and trust Gurpreet in a connection, the more her presence melts your inner blocks.

The connection can be as short as twenty minutes and as long as two hours: the length is at Gurpreet's discretion. During these connections, Gurpreet and the individual make eye contact and talk about the inner blocks or problems in their lives that are causing them stress (e.g., fear, anxiety, anger, loss, etc.). Her presence and words melt the person's heart and open the person to see his or her innocence and higher self. The transcripts of these connections have been taken from several retreats in 2011 and 2012. These connections have also been organized by subject matter.

Open Forum

In the beginning of every retreat session, there is a question-and-answer period during which Gurpreet answers questions on all subject matter.

Gurpreet's Journey to the Awakened Life

Why did you begin searching spiritually? Was there some event that happened to you, or was it gradual?

It was a combination of my own emotional pain and hearing about the concept of surrender. Death pain put me on this path. My cousin died, and shortly after, my husband passed away; and that put me on this path. There was such a huge fire inside of me to search for God. When my husband passed, it gave me freedom to move toward my fire and my search.

When I was thirty-three, I investigated an enlightened master's teachings for three or four years. I only read his teachings, and I listened to Osho's tapes. This drove me to search for a true teacher. I met my teacher in Edmonton, Alberta, and he put me on the path to self-realization. I had never met any spiritual teacher before, and in meeting him, my heart was lit up. It was like a yes in the heart, but I didn't understand what, why, or how. I knew something happened in my heart, and so I took one step at a time. I was with him for about six years.

For over four years, I had a really hard time understanding my teacher's language or knowing how to do the practice he was teaching. I was not really understanding very much of it at all. That created a bit of a setback for me, but it also opened me up to other side doors to spirituality.

In my third year, I explored other forms of spiritual awareness. I met a swami and many Sikhs, and I did lots of chanting mantras, meditation, etc. I met many different types of spiritual teachers. I met with astrologers, past-life therapists, and teachers of many other spiritual modalities in that year. I did many different kinds of meditation and applied everything I learned diligently. Then I realized none of it was really working. For example, chanting mantras softened my heart but did nothing more than that. I knew these techniques were not for me, and I knew they were not the true way.

So I went back to my teacher in Edmonton. The key thing I learned from him was to "stay in the pain." The other practices I had explored weren't about staying in the pain. When I heard this from my teacher, I knew there was truth in it, but I didn't know how to be in or stay in so much pain. Slowly I started realizing that something inside me would guide me. I loved being in my teacher's presence. I knew he was a powerful presence even though I had never met him in person.

How did your family respond to your spiritual search?

My family and friends were disappointed as I went deeper into my spiritual growth. My mother was very supportive of my search and is now very open to my teaching, and my father is very accepting also. My boys are twenty-seven and thirty, and I have a very open and lovely relationship with them. My sons love what I am. They recognize that I am coming from a true space. But my extended family and friends felt I wasn't the same way with them, which was true; their interests didn't interest me anymore.

On your journey, how did you stay in your heart while still working and raising a family?

For me, the unnecessary parts of what I used to do on the surface kept dropping away. My unnecessary dialogue with people, unnecessary activities, and unnecessary friendships kept dropping away as I saw there was nothing there for me. I took this on as my work, and in the beginning I had to remind myself many times that I wanted to do this walk. Slowly I developed a certainty that I needed to stay with this.

In my home life, my kids were with me and I offered them whatever I could, but I wasn't really controlling them. I stopped being fearful of where they were and what they were doing, hoping that such and such wouldn't happen—all that kind of dialogue in the mind about my kids. I gave priority to myself. Of course others didn't like that; they felt I was moving away from them. I gave priority to what was true for me. I tried my very best to give all of me to this walk. In the beginning it felt selfish at times, but I stayed with what was true in my deep.

Would you say that you have taken your teacher's teaching to a different level?

In some ways yes, but he did point me toward the knowing. I was really connecting, in deep awareness, to the inner knowing. Once I became deeply aware of the knowing, I moved quickly with that knowing.

Do you still see your teacher?

I did eventually get a chance to speak with him briefly. I love and value him. I love and value him; I don't need him, but I love and value him. I don't need to learn from him or see him, because I am not separate from anything now.

What led to your own enlightenment?

Pain—death pain of family members. When you are in death pain, there is no cure for it. There are no other doors to escape from that pain. Those deaths were my awakening toward this path. I realized that there was so much more to life than what I had been living. When I was young, I was not on any spiritual search. I was an ordinary wife, mother, and daughter—just very ordinary. After the deaths in my family, someone said to me, "You have never surrendered in your life." A lightbulb went on, and then I started searching by reading books, listening to tapes, and trying to practice and learn by myself. Then I realized I needed someone who could teach me, and through my teacher, I learned.

What teachings have brought you to the place you are in today?

I did have a thirst about what was beyond me. I had a strong pull. Through this pull I learned what was blocking me. I would ask myself, "Why can't I be my real self; why am I separate from it?" I realized that the created self stands in front of the real self. So I started recognizing my created self, which was my wants, needs, patterns, and beliefs. I can see this clearly in others now. When people—students—give me their true openness and not just a mental openness, this gives me permission to have greater access to them so they can taste where I'm at, little by little.

What was your biggest challenge in your journey to awakening?

I was in so much pain—extreme pain, and deep emotional pain. I was really being bent by my emotions. I would give myself to others in an emotional way, which caused me a great deal of pain. I couldn't see my childishness, my weaknesses, and my big emotional body.

What did you do with this pain?

I knew I just needed to be in it—to just let it come to me and learn to be okay in it. It took acceptance, and with that I began to have more clarity about my weaknesses. I began to stand in myself by being okay in my pain and by continuing to open my eyes, which brought clarity to me. That is why I teach people to enter the pain first, because that is the biggest protection in people—protection against their pain.

Do you socialize much now?

I keep changing since the awakening, so I only go where I really need to go in terms of family gatherings. It's not something I really long to do, but I go and do enjoy it a little. When I began walking toward awakening, I dropped socializing. A person on this journey becomes much straighter within, and others don't like that in social situations. Music and movies have also dropped away for me over time. Early in my walk, I watched movies to learn more English to help me expand my vocabulary. As a child I was not very verbal, and after the awakening I realized I didn't have a big enough vocabulary to be able to answer people's questions. I needed a larger vocabulary for people to understand what I was teaching.

You are always so well dressed and wear such lovely clothes.

My life now is more about shedding, but I always did like dressing well, even in childhood. And yes, even awakened I still appreciate clothes. But during the walk to awakening, I shed everything inside me. I completely dropped every tiny thing about self, and so now I am completely okay with whatever I wear and it doesn't matter if I look a particular way. A person has to lose attachment to his or her own appearance, clothing, and presentation; absolutely everything must drop.

Can you tell us how you knew you had awakened? Did it happen suddenly, or were you aware it was happening?

Yes, I knew I was getting close, but that closeness wasn't a mental understanding. I wasn't touching that at all; it was just more with myself about letting go. By the point I really knew, there was complete clarity. In the walk there are some stages where a shift comes and the person thinks, "Yeah! I got it!" But there is still some tiny question that stays, and that means the person is not yet home. When the clarity really comes, you completely know. It doesn't happen to everybody like that, though; that is just my experience.

One day you were not awakened, and the next day you were awakened. What was different?

All my questions, all my doubts, were dropped; I had unlimited clarity. That was the biggest difference.

What is your daily life like in the transformed state? What is your physical reality now?

The physical body changes when the grip of the mind is not always there. In my teaching I am always encouraging people to land more into their own self—to fall deeply within—because then they loosen up and let go of some of the mind's grip. Then they can be within. I personally went through many physical and emotional changes as I progressed. But now it happens so fast that I don't really notice myself shifting. I see my shifts happening in myself very quickly now. Intense pain comes in the very beginning because the person is holding back. People have to learn to be in their body, mind, and emotions and in pain physically, emotionally, and mentally. Slowly everything will move through their system.

What drew you to become a teacher once you awakened?

I had many glimpses of people coming to me, and I could see they would get purified through me while I was walking, but I kept ignoring these glimpses because I loved the walk so much. I wanted to die in the walk, but the visions kept coming. I didn't touch anything; I just said again and again to myself, "I want to completely diminish in this walking." Suddenly I found I had stepped into being okay with being a teacher. But I didn't control it; it wasn't something I tried to make happen in any way. People just started coming to me to talk to me about this walk. People would come, and I would have conversations with them about where I was coming from. Not everyone got it, but some did, and the ones who understood the walk wanted more.

What is your own inner connection like? Does this truth guide you and continue to guide you?

What I know and what I am—I am open in that. Saying I am the truth is too big to swallow. So I'm saying I'm just like you and I am open. I am completely open to you and whatever you are. I completely embrace whatever you are, and with that you can taste what I am. The more you can taste, the more it pulls you. This pull in you is something you don't understand, but that is the invitation for you to move forward. You don't need to understand what I am, but know that you can *be* what I am. Anything you label the truth will be too hard to swallow later on.

If something in you is touched by what I am, just go with that. Start with a little bit; it is easier if you can trust and then you can follow. The more you open, the more you will let me in. The more you let me in, the more you taste. The more you taste, the more your heart expands because your heart loves what I am.

Do you still go through shifts in your awakening or do you stay in constant bliss?

Awakening is not about being in bliss. That's not the only space you need to be in; there is more to discover within. You can still open up so much more inside you once you make the shift. I still move through raw and uncomfortable states at times. One just moves through everything.

In the beginning it was like the openings were one after another but with distance between them. Slowly the distance diminished, and I'm now in a flow that is happening very fast. Now I'm flowing, I keep moving through everything so fast that I don't recognize if there is any discomfort. In fact, I don't feel discomfort, because I'm not tight. I don't feel discomfort in shifts anymore, but I am aware that they are happening and that I am shifting. OR I don't feel discomfort in shifts anymore, but I am aware when a shift is happening and that I am shifting. I'm still expanding in my consciousness.

Do you believe in God?

That which is unknown a person will often call God. In my walk I still prayed to a higher power or the higher self. Recently that has disappeared because I am in nothingness now. Nothingness is just a beginning. It is a state of empty, zero, and yet it is very attractive. Right now I am in that space. Maybe I will change and there will be something different in the future. This is everything and this is nothing. It is whirling, attractive, broader, and I can see everything. It has every quality in it, and a person does need every single quality to recognize being in that nothingness. Where I am is very hard to describe.

How would you like to see your teachings expand into the world? What is your mission?

I don't have a mission. If the teaching ended today, I would be completely okay with that. I'm fine if it expands, and I am fine if it vanishes.

Seeing that you worked for your awakening in this life time shows that it is possible for us also. In my search, here and in India, the only awakened ones I met were so remote and so different from me. But you are so warm, natural, and accessible, and so easy to relate to. What was the biggest step you took toward your own awakening?

I began to understand what one really needed to do in order to be awakened. I realized that I had to face my inner pain. This was a deep and profound realization and a huge shift for me. Then I began to see my inner world—my impurities, wants, needs, beliefs. It helped me to turn the arrow toward myself completely. This was the biggest step I took. I teach that all the time; otherwise, we wouldn't know how to start.

I don't want people to have blind faith in me; no worshiping me. People are really tired of believing blindly and not getting any closer to waking up. They are deeply disillusioned. That's why I stress this is a direct walk about being direct with *themselves*. In the beginning people want to worship me or have blind faith in me, but if they continue to walk, they quickly see they don't need to do that. They just need to return, in a direct way, to their inner self. This in itself is a most beautiful thing.

You don't have to leave your home to go practice in a cave or a monastery. Those things are on the surface, and the surface has no meaning. It doesn't make any difference if you wear nice clothes or rags or a monk's robe. If you believe that is important, then that's holding (beliefs, attachments, desires, experiences, values, etc.), and that's dishonesty. This walk is about *seeing* what you are not willing to give up, what you think you need to hold on to in order to be spiritual and to be protected.

What can you tell us about how you are changing and how this will reflect in your teaching?

Up until now, in my teaching, I would go into the person sitting in front of me and experience what the person *is* in a direct way, but not anymore. Now I am flowing and have gone so far beyond that I don't need to do that anymore. About a year ago, I was feeling some type of shift and I told people, "I'm going to be different; these meetings will not stay the same." This wasn't boredom; I had ripened. I don't have to go where I did before; I will go beyond because I am different now. This is broader. These meetings may look or feel less intense, but actually they are more intense than before. I will only connect individually now if the person really needs it, but not otherwise.

8

I am so much more than what you are accessing right now. I do know what is true to be, and this change in format is not only about me; it's also about all of you. It's *your* need and not just my expansion. I know you can handle more of me and you can go further now.

Sitting with all of you right now, I am connecting with each one of you simultaneously. Initially for the first few years I thought I would work on one person at a time with the stillness. Now the intensity is so much stronger and is too much for an individual. In the past I had to go through different states of being. I needed to learn and to integrate in every way. I'm not missing anything now; everything is complete because I have integrated completely, the same as you are doing.

Many people have been taking my teachings in a very personal way; using the connections to "feel good." It's not about feeling good. This walk is about loving your smallness so you become less, less, and less and go beyond the way you have been perceiving the walk.

There is less need for intense individual connecting. It will just happen as required. Whatever is needed is always provided. This teaching and my way of being have always been and always will be from the higher self. In the new meeting format there will be more direct learning.

I am and have become natural, and I'd like to stay natural so the people learning from me can also stay natural. In unnaturalness there are still belief systems that aren't needed anymore. People come here for inner freedom.

In the beginning of my journey, I knew it was not just about energy, and I have been telling you this. There are still so many beliefs and a need to feel energy and to think that it is real. It is not real. The more people feel energy and believe in that, they won't face reality and face what is more valuable and what is higher. I have been explaining about people's experiences and how they can be played with, but any given experience is not always an awakening. When people grab an experience, they then begin to believe they have some realization and actually they are going blind again.

In reality, you don't feel. It's empty. It's clean. A person believes, "What I was looking for—I've got to feel something." That's why doubt comes to people. So I've been telling people, "Instead of grasping onto a tangible experience, be clean and pure, and as you become pure you will realize you have clean clarity within."

Somebody called it Fancy-land. People have the ability to build a Fancy-land, especially a spiritual Fancy-land. Being in Fancy-land, the person wants something, wants to grab onto something.

This isn't Fancy-land. This is *waking up* in a simple way. I know that people need to hear this again and again so they can come out from what they have believed.

Just be as a lover, and instead of wanting something or to go somewhere, just be present. *Be* what you are. People want infinite love, or want to be one, or want to be home; these are only intellectually fine names. Everyone thinks this is something *big*, but that is only imagination. People are caught in their own walls [beliefs] and keep imagining, "I want that; I want to be finer, higher." People close their eyes and try to calm themselves, and they try to find stillness. In all of these techniques, there is nothing there. People are using all their energy for no reason. There are so many beliefs. When you finally see reality, you just laugh inside. Reality is so *it*.

Remember, being here at the meetings and being in the presence really helps. When you bring one issue forward with honesty, then it easily disappears and your falseness falls apart. That's the meaning of *being* in the presence; it happens very fast and very quickly.

You say we are not to be dependent on you, yet I feel I have to be in order to keep walking and diminishing. Could you talk about that?

In the beginning you are, in a way, dependent on me *for* the higher self, which is never dependent on anything. You need me in the beginning to learn how to earn the knowledge within. It's not to depend on me; it is to love what I am. I'm taking you slowly and gently away from every dependency. When you experience the oneness with me on the higher level, that in itself gives you the freedom to go there, because it *is there*. By loving me, you learn to love yourself, and by trusting me, you learn to trust yourself.

This love is *so* rich that you don't need anything within or without; it has all the freedom in itself. There is no dependency on anything. All I am doing is encouraging you to open up your eyes and let yourself be in that. Then there is no individuality.

Part of me doesn't want the connections to change.

Instead of wanting to grasp onto something in this and in the way we have meetings, just love; just love to be in the longing. This love of longing is very different from wanting.

Since my eyes have opened to this journey, in my own experience, I've always loved it; my lover is just this, nothing else. Now and from the very beginning, I have always loved it in such a natural way. Even if you don't know what you're looking for and you have no mental clarity about what you're longing for, that is not important. You know. You know it is something so subtle, so simple, so *it*. Nothing else can satisfy you. Even each shift you have along the way cannot satisfy you; you still want to go deeper.

When you are being as a lover and loving this, this walk becomes easier. Some people are naturally like lovers. Worldly love doesn't satisfy you, but this longing like a lover—this is how I am, and this is helpful. Even when you feel changes physically, there is no need to make a big deal about them. Don't verbalize and don't analyze; that way you simply (not complicatedly) move through everything. The more you analyze something that you are experiencing, the more it grows into a hurdle.

My way of being shows all of you that this is very simple and very possible, and that it doesn't matter what your patterns or your circumstances are. It is still possible. Keep that fire alive—a strong fire. Even if you are strongly stuck in a worldly way, keep the fires blazing. And make effort to go into your fears.

Why are only a few people willing to do this walk?

Many have a longing, but their fear, lack of fire, distrust, stubbornness, strong attachments to the falseness, and more keep them away from this. The longing and the willingness to respond to the longing helps keep them here. A person's trust, even in a subtle way, helps them to stay.

Also, circumstances can bring you here. These meetings are for the people who are looking for the end, not for a taste of peace or a momentary experience of love. This is the end. Say to yourself, "Being here is my beginning and my end. Even if it is until my deathbed, it doesn't matter, no more postponing. I cannot leave until I awaken." On my walk, I had this kind of depth of need and longing. You make that kind of fire for the deep and for the need and longing inside you. Give all your trust and all your effort to see it all. This is good. This is great.

Sometimes I get physical sensations when I am here and wonder if that is a sign of change for me.

It is a habit to want to feel something, and the wanting creates this trouble. The person keeps trying so hard to feel something. Then it is about "Me and mine" and "I got it" and "I am receiving it." But the person becomes like a twisted rope; each strand of the rope is feeling the other, but inside the rope there is nothing. Wants are like this. So trust what is *not* tangible. You want to feel something occurring in you as you walk, but don't feed that, or else the thickness of the rope will become bigger. I see in you how you so want to feel something, but there is no reason to do that. Just love this. Simple.

I am concerned that if you change the format of the meetings, then maybe I won't continue to move forward.

These are your own doubts and fears. Instead, think about the love. You don't need anything. People have deep-rooted beliefs about energy because it's tangible. Trust what you know.

In my own spiritual searching, I was acutely aware that some teachers bring strong electric waves of energy. After a while I realized with truth that if there is no honesty, no purity; those energies won't work. In reality, purity is nothingness and this nothingness *is* something. It's the individual's own responsibility to be pure. Don't get stuck in the experiences. Whenever you experience something, it is just a form. Let it go. Be simpler; keep earning the purity.

Do we need a teacher or someone to help us go beyond to experience this nothingness?

People use the word samsara (the endless cycle of birth, death, and rebirth). These meetings are for getting out of that cycle. It is hard to go beyond without having someone (a teacher) who is firm and straight and who won't let you stop anywhere. Use this life for the freedom. No more hesitations and no more excuses. Keep telling yourself, "In this life, no more." And yes, you do need someone's presence who is out, outside of the created self.

Are we learning to connect back into who we really are while we are in the meeting?

Connecting with what is subtle within—this is the learning. Here we learn to reconnect with it. The mind is always trying to understand and keeps refining in an intellectual way. Everything can be so defined, but it's still mind, and there is no truth in it. If you keep going into mind understanding, you will feel separation because it is not about the mind. When you are in *it*; you click. That's not mind understanding, although the mind is also able to understand these teachings. Everybody has this, it's just that some are lost and don't know how to reconnect. When you are able to connect, there is so much more. You are learning how to reconnect here in the meetings.

Why is this type of teaching not in the mainstream?

Two things: First, not very many people are willing to do this walk. They want enlightenment, but behind it there is a self-agenda. Their beliefs are very deeply rooted. They want the good feelings but not the discomfort. Second, there are not very many teachers who do this type of teaching, because there is a cost to this work for the teacher also.

You have so much wisdom. Does it just come through you, or is it because you're expanding? Where does it come from?

You can see it in me, but I don't see that in myself. I see myself as a simple person. When people ask me questions, I know the answers because it is so simple. Once one knows that everything he or she is hanging onto is not real and knows that nothing is real, then what you believe has no complications. Then wisdom is everywhere.

One of the biggest doubts I have is that, outside of these meetings, I won't be able to stay connected with the presence that you are.

You don't know how to stay connected, but you can see clearly it's just a doubt. Just see, simply, this is just a doubt. Don't get wrapped up in it; don't participate in it. Doubt will walk with you all the way on this journey. The more you try to wake up, the louder the doubts will be. Those doubts are because the old person doesn't want to be lost or gone. The doubt's job is to occupy you and confuse you. It's very normal to go back into doubts. Doubts keep coming to everyone. Some doubts are loud, and some doubts are not; that's the only difference. Everyone goes through doubts all the time. Just learn not to participate in those doubts. Tell yourself whenever you see or hear them, "It's just doubt, and I'm not participating with it." With doubts, you don't know what to connect with, and that's okay. Just know not to participate with the doubts.

If a person is really willing to diminish, to go beyond the created self, then doubts come in sly, tricky ways. You may get sick and think, "Uh oh, not good energy here, because I just got sick!" Or maybe upsetting incidents will happen. There are lots of ways the created self tries to stay alive in you. You may think, "I am being selfish being here," but this is the only good kind of selfishness.

Even my longing to wake up doesn't feel good. Each time I come here, I feel my heart breaking in a new way.

Experiencing presence here does help in a big way. It will take you to the next level very quickly. Just remember to take one step at a time. Every time you come here, yes, it is heartbreaking and not what you were expecting. But every time you come here, the fire in you actually becomes bigger. Trust that; even though it might not feel good, keep coming because your willingness keeps moving you forward. In each step you take, what is required for you will be provided, even when you don't understand. The presence moves a person forward very fast. Just sitting here in the meetings, the fast-forwarding keeps happening. You won't understand what is happening, but it *is* happening.

Isn't the longing to awaken just another kind of wanting and needing?

The longing to be awakened does not come from the mind. It is not wanting or needing. It seems that way because mind understands that way. Longing comes from beyond; that is the reason a person often doesn't understand.

You can feel as though something is missing in the midst of everything you have. You are trying to understand, analyze, or run away from it. But nothing works, and nothing will work, because that missing piece is *you.*

The stronger the longing you have, the better. It is a true desire from the higher self. You realize you are no longer satisfied with all that the created self has accumulated: family, children, love, house, money, position, possessions. Even if you have everything you could have imagined; the created self cannot satisfy you once you realize something is missing. Only a few people are letting that realization awaken in them and begin the true search.

Being in the Walk

How does a newcomer begin this walk? How do I start?

First, come to the sessions as often as you can. This walk is not something you can understand with the mind; it's not something I give you. The presence you will encounter here is absolutely important. People need to sit in these meetings. Sitting here, you will grasp this understanding through the heart in a direct way. Generally the mind filters everything and twists and complicates it before it gets to the heart. But here in these meetings you can open your heart and learn to *be* in a simple way. Sitting in the meetings can be a challenge; your issues will come up, and your mind will say, "I really don't like being here," but your heart *does* like being here. Trusting the heart won't be easy to understand in the beginning, because you don't trust your heart in the outer world; there you only trust your mind. Make yourself come to the meetings, and slowly you will be able to see what is happening at the meetings. Your longing is the key.

What starts this type of search, and why are some so drawn to these teachings and others are not?

Any kind of pain is a signal to start the search. But if the person is so busy putting ointment on, trying to heal the pain or ignore the pain, he or she won't go into the deep. If you are not being satisfied with any answers, then you will be drawn to the pull. You don't need to satisfy yourself; pain actually takes you toward awakening. Pain is not bad. Some people are ready; some are not. It depends on the person's sleepiness. If you are too sleepy, you won't want to wake up.

You often speak about knowing. As I walk, I find there is something inside that says, "I just know this is so." Is this knowing changeable yet continuous?

Yes, it changes as you change. As you become clearer, you are able to connect with your inner knowing easily, rather than your mental perceptions. The knowing is not mental; the knowing is from the heart. By trying to understand more than that, you will give form to it. When you give form to it then again, it will become a dance.

I truly feel love for my mind because it enables me to accept whatever I am. Is this all right?

It is all right. Just remember that accepting your mind is not enough. Accept more than the mind. Accept what the mind has created.

✿✦✿✦✿✦✿✦✿

I am leaving Canada for my home. Can I do this walk on my own?

When you go back to your home, don't go to the place of satisfying yourself. Be in this pain that is pulling you. Be in the sadness, and feel that the world is finished—gone. *You* make it happen. Think of it this way: if you had a lover and then you separated, what would you ask for?

That we would meet again.

Remember the fire. True lovers never stay separated; they will pay any cost. Your pull to this is the strength you need. Never let this new beginning come to an end.

✿✦✿✦✿✦✿✦✿

I can see how judgmental I am, and how wrong I've been about everything and everybody. I thought I was better and ahead of everyone on this walk. I now realize that this was all ego talking.

You can see how your thinking is not clear, not clean, and not right. Be clear with yourself about what this is and what it is not. It's not verbally saying anything or confessing anything out loud. It's only you being naked and exposed *within* you. Always be kind regardless of how wrong you are, regardless of how much ego you have. This doesn't matter; just be in the acceptance that "this is me," with kindness.

❧❧❧❧❧❧

I am wondering how to do this walk with these problems I have. I take stimulants to get going and then antianxiety pills in the afternoons. I don't know how to get out of this cycle, and now we're having a second baby. I know this is toxic, but I'm not stopping.

The bottom line is that you have been avoiding the pain, and this started the cycle. You are in the cycle now and don't think you're smart enough to control or fix this. You are giving yourself a constant challenge—a challenge you are never going to win. Come back to the kindness of your heart. Don't fix anything you want to get rid of; you are giving it a challenge, and you will try to kill it. You don't need to kill anything in you; come back into you with kindness where you can be with yourself a little bit more, but not with your mind and not with your bigness.

The real peace you seek, you haven't found yet. See the innocence in your child and let it touch your heart. That is a tiny taste that your mind doesn't understand. This is in your heart, and you stay with it. Continue to go back again and again to what you taste in your heart, not in your mind. Be what you taste in your heart; learn to *be* in it. Otherwise you're going to start using your child to feel good—another dishonesty within you. That will be another dependency. Look within yourself in a kind way, very kind, and be in your heart. Right now you get high with self-judgment. The more you go high with those self-judgments, the more you think you can solve your problems. But it won't work; you're just creating more challenges.

So how do I start this walk?

Again you're looking for the Band-Aid, but instead, be in your wounds (see them, be aware of them, and embrace them without judgment) and feel what it brings up in you. Your wounds shows you the answer. It will show you how to *be* instead of avoiding. Your wounds will soften you.

I don't want to be in sorrow all the time.

You're making sorrow inside you anyway. Trust yourself. Your thinking is in the way. Choose to be in your wound with kindness and with gentleness. Be in the kindness always.

With my life being so busy, how can I get to that place of being in my wound?

You are choosing to make it busy. Don't live for your busyness; live for you. Let yourself rest within. Talking without acting on your longing is increasing the sense of your busyness. You keep protecting yourself with pills. The more you protect, the more you crave the busyness. You keep yourself high this way. Let yourself be less.

❧❦❧❦❧❦❧❦

Being on this walk has really shown me how asleep I am. Can you tell me why we are so asleep?

For many reasons: it's a familiar state, it's a matter of irresponsibility, and it's a desire to stay comfortable in sleep. Mostly we do not want to let go of the familiar even if there is suffering in it. We are not necessarily born asleep. A baby has a simple heart and has simplicity. But the identity begins, and that's where the trouble starts with our wanting and needing and having to have. The person shuts off the awakened self as he or she grows more of a created identity.

❧❦❧❦❧❦❧❦

How can I get out of my own way in this walk? When I meditate, I can't control my thoughts.

You are neglecting *you* by focusing on the mind instead of the heart. Don't worry about the thoughts; instead, kindly turn toward your heart. Even when you can't find yourself, at least you're not fighting with your thoughts. Learning to turn kindly away from your thoughts will slowly come. You will learn little by little. Working with your mind and your thoughts is not a bad thing; it's just that you confuse yourself because there's so much going on in your mind. This makes you even more frustrated, and you don't need that.

❦❦❦❦❦❦

Psychotherapy is built on the notion that the mind and emotions are connected and that healing comes by understanding which thoughts create which emotions. But your teachings are different from that.

Your system is trained to understand through the psychology of the mind, which is very limited. But don't try to take giant steps all at once. It takes time to shed belief systems. It takes time to learn how to rest in the waters of the heart. Just take tiny steps (slowly) toward this new way of being. Be content and rest in this. Trust in this. You don't have to block whatever your mind tries to make up; just let it rest, and don't touch it.

You say that the more you trust, the deeper you can go; is this the whole key?

Mind understanding is very limited. Trust is much more powerful and takes you deeper into pain. This walk is like a toddler learning to walk: first crawling; then holding on to objects, then a hand, then finally walking on his or her own. The amount you can trust yourself is earned. It is not a belief system; it's a knowing, and you know that with your heart. Trusting in me is really trusting in you.

What does it mean to love yourself, and how do I learn how to trust?

Generally people are very hard on themselves. They beat themselves up by covering, pretending, or trying to change themselves. When you let yourself crumble, you won't need to understand who or what loving yourself is. Let everything fall apart, because this will make you clear about your created self and your real self. You're not seeing your real self yet, but you are letting yourself see that you are the one who has created everything. The surface shows you this, but you don't need to hang on to it. The surface world is not stable. People hang on to jobs, money, children, partners, belief systems, and patterns. They create complications by leaning and wanting. The surface is visible, but the world within is not visible, and that's why you have to trust.

See that the outside world is not permanent. You do know that within you. Recognize that what you are hanging on to is not permanent. This is making everyone sad and lonely. That is what people run away from— sadness and loneliness. It's only hard because people don't understand. It's not easy to get out from your own grasping and avoiding. People think they are working on themselves, and they tell themselves, "If I can just understand it, I can work with it." This path is not that easy, because it's not about understanding. Rather, it's about learning to *be*, little by little, so you don't threaten your person. Just gently and kindly enter everything inside.

Is our sole purpose on this earth to awaken?

We're supposed to be awake! It is how you are meant to be. There is no need to suffer. There is a simpler way to be. You don't need to question why all this happened, its origins, the planet, or yourself. Just realize this is a beginning; it's a good thing. Be happy to begin to awaken.

Is it okay to do other spiritual teachings along with your teachings while on this walk?

Ask yourself how these other spiritual teachings are serving you, and then go with your knowing within. If you are hanging on to these spiritual teachings to stay busy or to avoid looking at yourself, then that is not okay. But if the inner knowing feels that these spiritual teachings are truly helping you to grow closer to your heart, then it's okay. Adding to mind knowledge is just another load that you will have to shed. Trust what you already know within you. Loneliness is better than being confused with other teachings. In this walk, each person is actually learning how to be alone and how to go into emptiness and aloneness and how to embrace it.

Does everyone have to feel despair and sorrow and heartache in order to walk this path?

As long as the person is busy running from the real self through achievements, marriage, children, and jobs, then the person has no time to see. But in life there can be a sudden, intense event, or a realization of longing, and this is when the person is torn apart. It is painful when people turn their face toward everything they have tried to cover up and have avoided by keeping themselves too busy to see. But each person needs to face that with delightfulness, with happiness.

You will feel the sadness, but you don't need to pile more sadness on top. Bring in a little excitement from your side. You don't need to be disheartened and throw yourself in the ditch. Bring kindness, delightfulness, and positivity while facing whatever you have created. Turning back into you is the most beautiful thing. You can make this walk beautiful by applying your positive qualities. Initially this walk is confusing because it is the opposite of mind understanding. You need to have trust to walk this journey—trust in yourself. It can feel confusing at first, but if you trust your love or your love of being in your heart, then it's an easier walk. In the love, you don't lose anything; you won't lose yourself in it.

Can you talk about the choices we have while walking on this path?

When you're walking on this path, with every step you take there will be more realizations about things not being real. With every step, you begin to realize the unrealness and the fact that you have no choice but to keep on the path. In worldly decisions, any choice is perfectly okay, but you have to learn to be in that complete okayness, and then there will be no issues arising. For example, you think you should go with your heart's choice, but you don't, and so you make the wrong decision, learn to be okay in that, and learn to embrace the choice you made as it is.

In worldly decisions, a person always asks, "Where will I gain more?" But on this path, you don't think like that; instead you're just okay with everything because you're just okay to lose. In this, everything will fall into the okayness because there will not be any wrong choices. Whenever you try to avoid something on the surface, it will come back again and again until you face it directly and completely.

So great is my frustration about coming or not coming here. I want to run away and give up, but also I am being pulled here. I find myself in this conflict all the time.

Value the pull. The rest just learn, little by little. The pull is your living water. The cost of it doesn't matter. The cost only matters when there is a lack of that pull. When you don't let the pull live in you, it will cost in *all* ways.

Also I feel almost panicked that I'm not getting this walk! Yet somewhere inside I know what you are saying is true.

It's more like you are learning unfamiliar things. And this is not done with your mental understanding; rather, it's a direct experience inside you. In society we are taught that all understanding comes through the mind in a mental way, and yet inside you *know* that understanding is soft and subtle; it's a gentle nod of the head saying yes. That is quite different from the mental way. *Trust* that soft and subtle knowing, because that is the true "getting it." That trust leads to the *real way*.

The person does not connect with the real self because the person does not trust the real self. But trust grows more when we say to ourselves, "I don't understand mentally, but I choose to trust that I really do know. I choose to be *in* it even though it's unfamiliar." Knowing that it's okay that you don't understand this with your mind, you can rest in your trust. Trust takes baby steps to develop.

❧❧❧❧❧❧❧

I feel like my inner self is so cluttered. How can I declutter so I can be with myself on this walk?

Just be okay with the clutter and *learn* to be okay in the clutter. You don't need to solve everything. Little by little learn to be *okay* in the clutter as life is going on around you. First learn to be kind with yourself even though you see so much clutter. Kindness and okayness will bring the little bit of restfulness in your mind and help you. In restfulness you may see your clutter even more, but it's okay. With trust you can go deeper. The trust comes from the okayness (just accepting everything as it is.)

How can I stay in my knowing and not get bent by other forces outside myself?

Recognize when you are bent. As you recognize this, stay in that knowing. First understand with the mind that you are being bent by outside forces. Stay within your heart, where you *do* recognize how you have been driven by other forces, and then let yourself feel. Let yourself feel the way it comes to you and whether it brings disappointment, sadness, etc. Just stay honest. Stay honest with the way you feel, and doing that, let yourself just *be*.

With all that surrounds us in our daily lives, how can we be in that presence without using our mind? I try to go back to being in the heart, but I am having trouble doing that.

You can be in the presence by seeing what is in the way and by seeing the creations of the mind. Ask yourself, "What is stopping me from *being* within myself?" You are trying to go into being with yourself, and the trying is getting in the way. This needs to rest and just see what you've created. Trying creates blockages, and beneath trying are other blockages.

Learning to just *be* is quite a process. (You need to see everything you have created.) Just *being* is not that easy, but it is possible. The little experience you've had of just *being* is inviting you, but this will be at the cost of the created self. There is a knowing in you, so lay your head in that. That's it. You know that you need to lose your person. So trust.

I am struggling with staying with this walk because of my family. My family is worried about me changing and not being the same person. Also I love this walk, but my family doesn't like me being away on the weekends.

When you completely give yourself to your thirst, the other challenges are secondary. When you are hoping for these challenges to get better, you are not being honest with yourself. Do your best to be honest in your longing for your walk. Don't get bent by other challenges. The more you bend, the more they will drive you. They drive you because of you. They drive you because of your fear, your wanting, and your avoiding. When you are living for what is outside of you, you will always go up and down. You don't have to feel cheerful, and you don't need to be controlled by your fear of losing. See what is being shown in you that you *can* see. The fear and guilt won't keep you in clarity. See through your fear, and see through what you are feeling guilty about.

✍❧✍❧✍❧✍❧

My motivation to work as much or as hard as I always have in the outer world is just not there now that I am on this walk. Do I let my work go?

Continue to look for what is true for you to be. You are going through a stage. It is a stage where you don't feel motivated to work as much as before. Don't spend time wondering *why*. Just continue to work, continue to delve within, and you will integrate through your work. Allow yourself to change within. Keep a steady course in this, and slowly your inner self will show you how to *be* in it. And yes, it's true, as we go through the changes to self-realization, many things do become more difficult in many ways. This is normal.

So are you saying not to draw any conclusions, stay steady within and see what happens, and not make any decisions to drop my work?

Yes, exactly. In one way your life will become much simpler, and in another way it will be harder because you won't know how to integrate being simple. But don't make an issue about it, because then you will become involved in the mind. Just let yourself move through it. Just see.

Could you speak about being direct vs. indirect?

Let's say you are having a painful conversation with someone. If you are soft in the heart, you'll feel the pain inside you. What happens is that the mind kicks in and you create a story about the other person: "Oh, they are not good. They are not honest. They should be doing this or that." Now you are compromising yourself and protecting yourself with the story. The initial pain is direct. It pierces the heart, but the story is indirect.

Why does this walk bring so much heart pain and heartache?

When you don't embrace the pain and label it as bad, you close yourself off from it because it seems to be too much take, but in reality, there is no pain. In the beginning it's like pushing the energy of the pain through a narrow channel, and it is intense. But if you take down the walls of the channel and open up the constriction, the pain has a lot of room, and then there is no pain.

When I am in your presence, my heartache is so much easier to handle. Why is that?

Because your walls are down. When you are by yourself, you unknowingly put the walls back up.

How can we actually be with our pain without creating more walls?

Learn little by little. Initially you think, "Let me understand, and *then* I can do it." But in every moment, dishonesty is tricking you. The main thing is to be okay with the pain. But that is not easy when you have a habit of protecting yourself. Self-protection works in such hidden and secretive ways. That's why I keep telling you to come to the sessions so you can see your walls. We do a lot of protecting against our pain by keeping active and busy. Start with whatever you are thinking about.

Don't manufacture labels and impose confusion; just be with whatever you are feeling. If you feel pain, start with pain; if you feel protection, start with that. You don't need to change yourself in order to be real. Recognize and accept your habits, and then you will slowly be able to be free yourself from your habits.

❦❧❦❧❦❧

I can never make a decision, and then I get stressed out. How can I just go with the flow of life?

The surface shows you what obstacles you have in you. When there is nothing solid at the surface, it's just there *as is*; it becomes formless. That means there is no solidness driving you, no force driving you. When there's no force driving you, everything becomes easy and simple as it is. It's the person who makes it complicated. "Should I or shouldn't I?" the person asks over and over. That's too complicated. Instead of debating all the time, face the reality that is clear. Whichever side you choose, you are still able to *be* in the honesty as long as you're not driven by your decision. *Love* your walk and let your heart be in love. Love *every* way you walk. Even love what has opened up in you. Let your heart stay in the warmth of this opening.

At times I am not sure if I'm in my heart or tricking myself with my mind, and I become paralyzed.

You don't need to paralyze yourself. When you are paralyzed it is because you're being too tight with yourself, putting yourself under too much stress. When you are comfortable, then you are not doing anything; you are just being with yourself, being comfortably aware. Then you will know where you are.

Instead of controlling your inner world, just let yourself see, and then deepen your rest within you. When you do this, you will trust yourself more and you can ask yourself if there is any truth in this. If there is untruth, stand in it. If there *is* truth, then just go ahead. When you are in the deep, you know. But the question for you is, do you like to trust your deep? When you trust your deep, your surface will shatter. That is the cost. If you pay the cost of the old, you can move into the newness. Trying to hang on to the old makes it hard to move in the newness. You only hang on to the old when you don't trust the newness within. You don't need to go anywhere to do this walk; you don't need to go to a jungle or a cave or anywhere away from your experience in the here and now. Our created self is deeply hidden, and because of this we make it very complicated, but it really is very simple.

Sometimes it's easy enough to realize I've fallen, but it's not so easy to get back up.

Often when you are falling it is because you are trying. So each time you fall, you must recognize what you are doing. Are you returning to trying? If you are trying, it's not going to work. Every fall is teaching you something new. There are so many ways you can participate, so every fall can be useful. Remember to stay kind and gentle with yourself.

So you are saying that it is okay when I fall, but I should just be kind to myself.

Yes, but don't turn your face away. Stay in the awareness of your feelings. If you're not touching your feelings or playing with those feelings, then they will really open up and give you lots of room for them. You will see that they won't harm you, and slowly they will go away.

Are you saying that we should return to the innocence we had as a small child?

Yes. Since childhood, you have been walking away from home, away from yourself. Finally you realize you want to go back home, and now you have to go back through everything you have created along the way. You cannot blame anyone else; there is no justification. You have to go back and melt all that you have created to return to the innocence.

What should I do when I feel happy?

Stay grounded in it. You need much more awareness in happiness, and you need to learn how to stay grounded and not fly away in happiness. Being grounded makes your own ground softer. It is perfectly okay to feel happiness and perfectly okay to feel sadness. Just let yourself be in both of them, but remember that both of them are not for you. Notice happiness is there; let yourself feel it and be in it, but don't touch it. In this you don't need to grasp or run away from anything. Let it be. Let yourself be softened in it.

❧❦❧❦❧❦❧

I feel guilty that I'm not doing enough for my family while I am on this walk.

Not accepting yourself and your guilt doesn't do you any good. With acceptance, the baggage will be put down. When you accept in an honest way and let yourself feel whatever guilt you are feeling, *that* allows you to be in that beingness, and then you can see your fear more clearly. Let yourself lose what you are not letting yourself lose. Fear means you are holding. By doing this, you make everything complicated inside of you. By letting yourself *be* in this, you'll gain a little bit more clarity and won't be driven by your fear and guilt.

When I am away from the family on some weekends, I feel guilt.

Keeping that belief is too much work. You don't need to carry that belief in any way, regardless of the situation at the surface. Let that belief shatter in you; let it hurt you. At least you are honest with it and not doing any labor to hold on to that belief you have. That can rest, and then your fear and guilt can also rest. When you don't let your fear and guilt rest, you give them power and they drive you. Your doer-ship needs to diminish in all ways. When the heart bleeds in the pain, it's much better than too much dust in the head, which gives power to the dust of fear and guilt. When you are in the dust, you create more dust, and when you are in the real ache of your heart, you expand—you open more than before.

Is it the longing for the real self that we are striving for on this walk?

You won't feel longing all the time. You start your walk with longing, and as you walk, you face many different states. When you feel like you're trying to satisfy yourself in the outer world, then you bring back your longing. You don't need to satisfy yourself anymore. That longing will continue to help you to have a fire-full walk. Have the desire for the love to never diminish. It does get cleaner and purer as you walk.

Is this walk for both the discomfort of facing my created self and for the trust that I can go deeper?

It's for the discomfort; distrust is already there. But *choose* to trust always with the trust you gain. That gain you won't understand, even when you think you understand with the mind. The trust is always fresh. With every step, you'll gain more alertness, so do not participate with the distrust too long. When you are participating, you are completely blind. The more you love, the more you trust and the more you will stay in the pull. It becomes a little easier.

Why is it so hard to stay on this walk?

Because you are so used to walking in one direction. You've been walking millions of miles in one direction toward your home, and then suddenly someone tells you, "Go back; your home is the other way!" Your system is not used to the opposite direction. You've believed for so long that every step you took was in the right direction, but now the direction has changed. It's heartbreaking. You are losing all the miles you've discovered, and it doesn't feel right, and because it doesn't *feel* right, you now need to trust someone who can walk you back. As you trust someone other than yourself, you will also *know* in the deepest part of you that it is right. Thus, you will slowly let yourself trust in what you know is truth.

In a past connection I had with you, you told me that there is no forward or backward. What do you mean by this?

Beingness means there is nowhere to go either forward or back. If you think you are going somewhere, you are disconnected from self and going outward, which means you are putting effort outward. On this walk, stay within and be in your dishonesty. If you are in discomfort, stay in it. There is no forward and no backward and no goals. Let yourself see more so you can *be* more. Let whatever happens happen; don't lose yourself because you're "going somewhere" with this.

✦❧✦❧✦❧✦❧✦

I'm noticing my resistance and my stubbornness and my not wanting to move quickly through these changes on my walk. It's like I'm a donkey with its feet braced.

Willingly be in the resistance. You are seeing another part of you. Say to yourself, "Okay, resistance and stubbornness, you need to come over here now." You don't need to change the resistance or stubbornness, because you're already seen these parts. Even though at first you only get a flash about them, you are still seeing the donkey. It's okay to be in that blockage and let it open up in you. A lot is opening up in you, and that is why this resistance is coming on so strongly. Be kind—very kind—and very willing.

When you tell us to "land," do you mean land in the body?

No, land in the heart. This walk is about seeing a little bit at a time and then *being* in it. Be in the heart, and then you see a little bit more, and then you *be* with that little bit more that you see. Don't land in your mind or in your thoughts. If you try to collect all the information about how to do this walk, you won't go anywhere. People deal with their life this way; they collect all the information until they are comfortable that they now know exactly what to do. But in this landing in the heart, there must be *trust*. If you trust, it's easy to walk. This walk is not about getting or meeting God; this walk is about dying. This idea of becoming

God, getting God, or realizing God is going to shatter. You can go into this dying easily, or you can give yourself a hard time.

This walk costs. It has been costing me my social life and, in some ways, my family life because I don't want to have surface interactions anymore. I want to protect my integrity, but not at their expense.

When you are moving through so much within, you don't know how to deal with what's outside of you—*yet*. But when you settle down, you will learn little by little the true way of being with others. Sometimes you feel like you're crashing, and this can keep you in the smallness, but that's good. Crashing grounds you in the truth. Stay very small, very gentle, and very kind.

As I'm learning this new way to walk, sometimes it's as if I become water, having no hands and no legs. It's unnerving at times.

You feel like this because you are losing the familiar self. You are relating with everything in the world in a new way, and it is challenging. Don't focus on how you are relating with others on the outside and how that is changing. You can lose the honesty that way. Be gentle and kind with your changes however they show themselves. First do that.

I have learned so much from you over the years. But many times I feel I am still the same.

You feel the same because as you change to your real self, you become that. It's seamless. These changes won't be *seen* as much; you just gain a knowing inside. If you are looking for results, that means you are looking for something. Instead of looking for results, give yourself more to your walk. It is okay to feel you are both changed and the same. Trust that which helps you to trust, and don't participate with distrust. Distrust is going to walk with you all the way down to the deepest parts of you.

Yes, whenever there is a change, I feel it requires much more trust than usual to be in that.

Exactly. The changed state is very fragile.

There have been times when I felt that I lost touch with this teaching and I became disconnected. Sometimes I don't remember the teachings. Does this happen?

Yes. When you are more in the heart, your memory will not be like it used to be, especially when you are walking toward this new way of being in the world. Many times you can experience blankness, and in such cases you won't remember the teachings. That's why these talks and these meetings help so much.

Sometimes I feel quite disheartened and negative.

Now you know that you don't need to push that negativity aside. Be a kind friend with your disheartened feelings. This is how you catch your secrets from yourself, and every little secret is worth being in. When you're completely okay with being in the "bad books," there is honesty, and in this honesty you never need to be in the "good books." Open your heart to the disheartened feelings from every angle.

There can be a lot of drama in my outside surface world. Sometimes I feel fear, and sometimes I feel anger, and these emotions sweep me away. Should I try to be with all these emotions as they arise?

Just remember that while you are in the drama of the outside world, you still need to see you. When you see you, you'll be disappointed. That is worth being in, even if there are too many things coming at you at once, such as anger or fear. Stay with the emotion that is the most uncomfortable at the time. Let yourself go deep until you can really see how *you* created that emotion. Being responsible means staying, day and night, with one emotion at a time, as well as enjoying being in it and valuing it. At least you are seeing it, and this is good. Before these teachings, you would just get angry and touch on it lightly and then move away from it. But now you don't need to cover what you are feeling. Even if you lose the feeling, invite it back until it really opens your heart and takes you deeper.

Anything you *want* is a good place to start, because a want means that fear, anxiety, ego, and protection will start curling up around that want. In reality, love doesn't want or need anything. The created self always wants more; it wants more and more love, and there is dishonesty underneath that. This is not love; this is wanting. This is using something to feel good, to satisfy you.

Is it okay to feel good for a while, or do I need to always be digging and be in pain?

As long as you stay grounded in feeling good, you have earned feeling good; but as soon as you begin to use it, you start flying in it. Feeling good requires more responsibility.

I see that happiness turns into sadness because we try to achieve good feelings and then grasp onto them. There is a constant fluctuation between the two emotions. Can you tell me more about this?

Yes. When you are happy, you are flying, and when you are sad, you are falling down; you are leaning on one or the other. Just embrace both of them. Don't stay personal with it; just like it and notice it is there, but don't participate in it. Slowly you will be able to go beyond your happiness or your sadness. Slowly you will begin to go beyond and see a higher purpose beyond just being happy or sad.

What am I supposed to feel in "embracing"? Do you mean I generate loving feelings for my patterns?

Initially people on this walk are trying hard to find some ground through feeling happy, ecstatic, sad, etc., but in this there is no ground. Every step is a new fresh step to be in, and every step is different from the one before. Initially you think, "I've got it, I've got it." But keep walking, and slowly you get used to saying, "I don't get it; I don't know where the ground is." Begin to trust; just walk with the trust, and the more you trust, the faster you move.

What is my homework? What should I do next?

Listen to your connection many times every day. (Connections are taped and can be listened to at a later date via a private website.) Then create your own will. When you have no will, then you are being driven by other people's will, just like a ball being kicked and played with. Remember, this is because of you, not others. Be serious for this walk, and you will grow your own tree. Now you know your homework.

Having a Connection with Gurpreet

Could you explain what you are doing when you are having a connection with us?

It's not like I'm *doing* something. It's about *being*. I'm coming from a space where I'm *being* with each person as is. The person can use me as a mirror to see himself or herself, and he or she can also merge with the space I'm in. It is difficult to describe, because it cannot be explained to the mind or understood by the mind. The person is learning to trust, slowly. The more the person can trust, the stronger our relationship becomes and the more the person benefits from it. It's about the real self; it is about what you really are. That is beyond mind understanding. But whenever a person is curious about the real self, I can answer that.

What happens in these connections that move people forward? Are they transmissions of some sort?

Everyone will experience something unique. They may feel something happening, or they may not feel anything, but it is happening anyway. The presence and the clarity directly help you in such a direct way. You may not want to go into the deeper self; it feels dark and threatening. But I can be a mirror, a friend, a helper, a push. It depends on what you need. You can take my hand to go into your deeper self.

How can we allow this to manifest on a deeper level when we connect with you? What attitude should we bring?

You don't need to think about anything. Just let yourself be connected. If thoughts come to you, it is okay. The more you stay connected, the better it is for you. It is okay that you come here full of issues; just stay connected.

In a connection, are you actually experiencing our pain? Do you see where we are at and then help us move forward?

When I am connecting with people, I am not connecting from a mental plane. I'm just connecting from what I am. This is what I am. When I am connecting with people, I hold the space they are in. In holding the space, it becomes like a mirror to them. They are then able to see themselves and what they actually are. If they are not able to see themselves clearly, I can direct them as they ask me questions. I see where they are holding tight or not holding and if there is realness or unrealness. I'm not connecting with their thought process. Some people may feel threatened by the thought that I might be reading their thoughts, which I don't care about at all.

Can you speak to the differences between the connections in meetings and these open forums?

The connections are real work, and they are very intense. Sometimes people, especially newcomers, feel frightened in the meetings. In the connections, I am actually taking each person inside myself. These open discussions are a good thing to have, because in them I freely converse like any other person. You may get some deeper benefit from these open dialogues, of course, but in the connections I see people really go into the deep.

When I'm in your retreat, I feel like I'm in a dream state. I'll close my eyes and go into a most comfortable state; it's almost like napping but not really.

The lifestyle you've been living is so full of stress that being here relaxes you to such a point that you can hardly open your eyes. This level of relaxation is something you don't normally experience. There *is* an energy in the room also.

When you look around at each of us at the beginning of connections, what do you see? Do you see yourself as one with us, or are we separate?

I keep changing because I'm not staying in one stage. The way I am with people is changing also. I connected more with people in the beginning because there was still form in me. That is changing in me now, and sometimes I don't know *how* to be with each person, because I am less solid now, and as I grow, I lose form. Everyone is in my care, and I am offering myself to each person, and they can use me and can be with me. Sometimes I am not so much connecting as much as I'm just *being* with the person. I'm not experiencing *with* the person, but I am there for him or her.

What you just said is so profound. So we shouldn't hide from you or be shy or embarrassed. We should just open up and trust.

Yes! Everybody is exactly the same. We are all the same; we have the same core issues, the same feelings. Only the surface appearance differs. Inside, in the heart, we are the same. We are one. There is no you, me, or them; individuality is only at the surface. In reality there is no individuality; we are all one from the root. This is a way of becoming one again. Some people are naturally deeper, some more kindly. Everyone's patterns differ; that is where you are uniquely different from each person.

Where I am coming from is a state of moving and shifting, faster and faster now. The best way for me to talk with people is for them to ask me a question and allow me to answer it. If you don't ask a question, then for me there is nothing.

Are you saying that something needs to be initiated from our side to have a response from your side?

It's helpful if we converse or you ask questions, because then I can pinpoint something for you to look at. It also depends on your willingness, at any cost, to open up and see within yourself. I won't force you to look at anything or make you open up. That willingness comes absolutely from you. It is your openness and desire to receive this help.

In our last connection I was aware of shaking inside—a lot of shaking. What was that?

You went very deep in your last connection in Toronto last month, and the body isn't used to it. Also, your patterns and everything in you is shaken up. Where you went is new. But you did allow it. That's good.

Learn to live in that newness little by little. You know now that you are able to go deeper. As you change, your body will experience lots of things. The body changes as you change. Your body is going to be much healthier than it has been.

Are there changes at the DNA level? Are you a different person physically than you were before?

Yes, completely.

✎❀✎❀✎❀✎❀

It appears you are in a trancelike state. Are you channeling?

No. This is not channeling. This is the way I am. I am opening my space to others to walk with them, and I am able to be with them. I am not a medium. It is more like I'm opened up to everything in me. It is like doors are continually opening and walls are falling constantly. What is left? No walls, no doors, nothing. But that is hard to understand with the mind. The mind tries to understand this, but it is not possible.

Sometimes I feel like I can't handle what I see in myself as I walk this path.

Everyone has those times. They may think, "I am getting worse coming to these meetings." But the thing is, the lid is being lifted and everything is coming out. It's okay. It's nothing to be scared of. There is nothing to run from and nothing to get rid of. When you feel so overwhelmed by all that you are seeing, just stay in the meetings.

✎❀✎❀✎❀✎❀

In my connections in the past, I could go very deep and see things about myself that I hadn't seen before—many new patterns and belief systems. But now I feel like I've lost a connection with the outside world, and yet in a way I feel much more connected. I doubt what I feel sometimes.

Now you're connecting more and more with your inner and losing the outer. The inner is unfamiliar, but you know in your heart that your connection is more than before, even though you're losing the surface

39

connection. The way you connected the very first time—you have no doubt about that at all! Distrust is not in your way. As you go deeper, whatever is hidden in the deep will come up to the surface. This shows you more of you. Whatever things get in the way, including your habits, let them open up in you one by one. Every part of you deserves to have this connection. You never need to control your heart.

It can be hard to give real permission (trust) to allow you to melt our heart and to help us make permanent inner change while in a connection with you. Is this because we are protecting ourselves?

Yes. People are so accustomed to protecting their inner self by erecting walls around uncomfortable feelings that those protections have become automatic and unconscious. So they can say in their mind, "I'm offering myself; I'm giving you permission to enter," but that's not enough. That offer is not enough. Instead people really need to see themselves and how they are distrusting, how they are protecting. Everyone has a whole system of beliefs that basically say, "I really need to protect myself."

Everyone who comes here is still outward, trying to *do* something, trying to change something, trying to *fix* something, no matter how much spiritual work they have done. This way is different because you are moving *through* the created self but not by doing anything, not by fixing anything. Coming to the meetings softens each person, little by little. This happening is beyond the created self. The real self loves this; the created self does not. The created self suffers, and the real self is completely unaware of its suffering. But your love and trust are what make it all possible for you.

ৠৢৠৢৠৢৠ

I am seeing my darkness in me, and I want to run away from here. Can you help me understand this?

When you see your own darkness, choose to stay in the darkness and don't run away from it. Running from your own darkness is what makes you want to run away from these meetings. Your tiny willingness to stay with it—that is the trust; dearly hold that little bit of trust that is inside you. When you don't run from your own darkness and continue to bring yourself into the darkness all the time, that will show you how to keep the arrow toward you. You don't need to hope or manipulate yourself to change, because that means you're running from the darkness.

Would I be able to see my weakness in that darkness?

First things first. It is not a small thing for you to be in your own darkness all the time. You're already seeing how much disturbance is coming, because you've had a little taste of your darkness.

✿❀✿❀✿❀

When I am in a connection with you, you look so beautifully innocent!

When people connect with me, they experience many different things. Mainly you are seeing yourself. It's like I am a mirror and you are seeing something about you. Of course you don't understand with the mind what is happening, and it seems very strange. It's okay if you express this as we are connecting. In a direct connection, tell me what you are seeing, and I can direct you in the right way. But you don't need to understand or wonder why this is. Just let yourself be delighted.

✿❀✿❀✿❀

In your presence, especially in a connection with you, this delight you speak of is there. But once we go back home, how can we sustain this delight?

You *think* you don't carry the moment that you experienced with this presence, but you do. There is something that you do know. For example, you may eat something *so* sweet that you can't explain how delicious it is. It's that kind of resonance that stays in you.

Whatever you see in the connection is a form of homework. There is so much for you to *be* after the connection, and that is your responsibility. Remember, this is not just about me. I am teaching you that you can be whatever I am. This is all about you standing on your own two feet. You come, and you merge with me, and I merge with you. After your connection with me, there is so much for you to learn to be in. It's a lot! I am teaching each of you simply "how to be." In this process of learning, you will get it and fall, and get it and fall. I'm showing you how to stand back up again. It's so possible as long as the person is willing to pay the cost.

I want to stay connected with that little taste of sweetness and that love I have when I am in my connection with you, but it doesn't last when I leave you.

When you're trying to taste that sweetness and love, always *remember* the taste. You do that by facing toward the taste instead of searching for it or grabbing for it. Face toward what you've tasted. It depends on how honest you are being and the degree to which you are moving forward in remembering the taste. Honesty is always required. Don't give it to your mind. Your mind tries to grab it by saying that it knows what it is. Instead, go back into the heart with honesty and with little baby steps. There is nothing to get or grab; it's *being* with it cleanly. It's natural that you want to capture it, to know it and have more of it, but that is the old way. The new way is soft and subtle. It's okay; you don't need to understand or ask yourself, "What should I do?" Don't worry, and keep seeing if you are trying to grasp at this again. Then just rest; just be by staying still.

The Created Self
and the Real Self

Is the created self the same thing as the ego?

The created self is not *only* the ego; the created self is a whole bundle of all our beliefs, wants, needs, patterns, habits, and protections. Some people don't have a big ego but have a strong created self. Everyone has all of these parts, just in various degrees. Our families, our work—these things show us our weaknesses. But how to be in a weakness—that's a process. You have to earn your courage to move through pain, and you have to earn your abilities to be with your weaknesses. This is a process.

How can we understand our mechanical created self?

You cannot. You cannot understand everything at once about being mechanical. You can only see a little bit at a time. Learn to live in that little bit first, and that will show you the next little bit. The little bit that you know right now is that you are stuck and you are suffering. It's not about only feeling the peace; it's about needing to be awakened in your weaknesses and see what is driving you. For example, if you can see that you are carrying guilt from the past, that's a good place to start.

Looking for a little bit of peace or relief won't let you walk toward the complete truth. That will only let you walk for a couple of miles, because you will feel a little bit freer from your misery and so you will stop looking. But that is the worst tranquilizer you can give yourself. Live to be awakened to the truth and no less than that. That way you do not satisfy yourself anywhere as you walk, because you know there is always more and that more is endless. It is a good sign that you are able to see your suffering.

Why do we suffer? Is it the created self causing us to feel pain?

The suffering starts when people are living for the surface and living for their wants and needs because of their beliefs. We have been born with the seeds of control and fear; that is why people get wrapped up in all of that. Being wrapped up in anything on the surface is very easy to do, and in doing so, people make their lives mechanical. They are then no longer aware. When people are not aware, then slowly the real self becomes more and more submerged. People in this state are just sleeping and keep thinking, "Oh, I am really awake and doing what I need to do." They do *not* know what is lacking, because they are already in mechanical behavior, which continues to drive them. Your real self has no say in the matter, because you don't let the real self live. That's why letting the real self live will cost the mechanical self. Being mechanical is everything you have created—your guilt, fear, and wanderings.

Are we supposed to have the intention to lose our created self to the higher self?

The real atman (higher self) is always there. It's the created self that is covering it up. So trying to go directly to the real self won't work. The created self is always wrapped around the real self because that comes first and because the created self is *also* hidden. The person is not awakened in the created self, so the created self cannot recognize the real self. Recognizing the created self is quite challenging because it is hidden and it's also tricky. It really does not want to leave. What one needs to learn first is how to be in the created self in a liking way; a friendly way. The walk into the created self takes you home. Don't run away from the discomfort in losing the created self. It cannot come all at once, but one needs to learn how to do this.

Can you explain more about what the real self is?

The real self cannot be explained, because it has no form. It is beyond your sensory body, your emotional body, and your perceptual body, but at the same time it is everything. As you journey, you may experience times of blissfulness and you may experience everything in the outer world as *very* alive. That is a form, and you earn that by your trust and your thirst, but then you must let it go. You might even experience all-encompassing love and be in love with everyone and everything; but that too is a form that you earned, and that too needs to be let go. All forms that are earned must be let go as you move toward the real self. It just *is*.

Does grace have any part to play in finding our real self, or is it solely up to us?

You need a teacher who can tell you where you're "stuck" in your walk, and very few teachers are capable of doing that. Being stuck can be very tricky. It can give you the completely opposite message, because losing your way does not feel good. Being in the blissfulness is not hard at all, but if you have the true longing, it does not satisfy you. Your inner self always knows this is not it. And when you continue to trust that inner self, it will let you connect more and more in your knowing.

Why are we not real in the first place? Why have we come to live in our created self?

Being in a physical form is important because in this form, the person is complete in every sense of the word. Because we are born into that complete physical form, we have the ability to discover the real self so that we can merge back into our real selves. That merging back, explained in a simple way, is like making existence brighter. That's what your physical form is for. You cannot understand this, and you don't need to understand this. Your thirst and longing are enough to walk in this. This walk is just a return to the real self. That returning back is possible when a person stops satisfying himself or herself anywhere on the surface. Satisfactions won't let the person grow. The person has to be willing to go into the deep.

Are you helping us discover our real self through seeing our created self?

It's acceptance of the created self that lets you *be* in the real self. Start facing yourself and whatever is bothering you the most first. Some people start with love, and that's okay too. You just need to be willing and open to face everything in you, even though it gets uncomfortable. The stronger your thirst, the better you are able to go within and walk within and move through each thing as it arises. The thirst enables you to keep going even when your created self says, "No way, I don't want to face this." The thirst for the "living waters" will reply, "It is okay; I don't mind going through this."

When you reach your real self, does every challenge in life dissolve?

Yes, in a way. This is so hard for the human mind to understand. It's hard to answer that question. The human mind may think that it will be in some kind of space where nothing touches it. And in one way this is true, because everything is able to move through you, and in moving through you, it doesn't damage you.

Is the real self the heart, and is the mind what you call the person?

Actually when we start walking this path, we talk about the heart because there is so much directness in that. As you learn to be in the heart and become purer and purer inside, eventually everything is going to become heart, including your mind, and then there will be no person. That comes much later, not in the beginning. In the beginning you only see your impurities, continuously.

Okay, I understand about the heart now, but how do I understand the person or what mind is?

Any want or need or any kind of ego is all from the person. But you don't need to understand what is mind or what comprises the person. Just see in yourself, "Oh, this is ego, this is an attachment, this is a want, this is a need, this is a belief, and this is a pattern." Just see it that way. It makes it easy for me to call it "the person" and for you to understand what that means. That way it leads to clarity. Otherwise you are going to confuse yourself. See everything you need in a simple way.

What do you mean by surrender?

To surrender means to do it with the full warmth of your heart and to willingly embrace who you are in your unrealness. A different meaning of "surrender" is like when you say, "I give up. I can't take it anymore." Then you go into depression. That's not surrender; that's depression. The warmth of your heart is very important. That you will learn. Everyone is so familiar with the word "surrender," but they don't know how to surrender. In the meetings, you learn little by little how to surrender. It doesn't matter how strong your mental body is or how much you are in the mind, your heart still knows. Your heart is fine and soft.

When we are connected to the real self and we feel bliss, is it okay to embrace it?

It depends how honest you are within. If you are not honest within, the dishonesty can use that blissfulness to feel good. If you are not honest within, bliss can close the doors that you want to walk through. Blissfulness feels very good, but it is still temporary. The person always needs to work on being in that blissfulness and, while there, recognizing the prison of that blissfulness. You don't need to be in any kind of prison. When every prison disappears, effort and doing will also diminish completely. That is the real beingness.

When you reach the real beingness, that fully realized state, is there a natural law that has the power to bless you, to give you great awareness?

This state is not only *one* thing. It's not like you park yourself somewhere. It's like a continuum. Each level has many different levels that keep opening up. You are not in *one* stage. If you are in one stage only, then you are parked and trying to avoid everything *now*. This walk is a continuous opening up. At the realized stage, you are not totally in the body anymore, so you have the opportunity to continue to move and open up more. The realized state is not one thing; it's not one level, and it's not one state. It is a continual opening up.

ℐ✿ℐ✿ℐ✿ℐ✿

You often tell us to be in someone else's feet. What do you mean?

Being in the feet means not trying to understand or analyze someone else's state. Instead you are simply respectful, humble, willing, and honest. Being in the feet shows you the deepest in you. When someone hurts you, be in the hurt and see your own weakness. You can do this by staying with it, by not trying to understand it, and by not going into the other person with blame. Your beingness lets you open up and you see how *you* started it. You're not trying to understand the other person *or* yourself. You can tell yourself to *be in* the feet or *be in* the heart, whichever makes the most sense to you.

How do we diminish to the point where there is no more attachment and no more doing?

Honest willingness is the first step. Be willing to see your own holdings. Anything you can honestly see and be with will take you there. Continue to go back, seeing directly into yourself. Let every single holding open up. You don't need to let go; just allow your honesty to say that you won't touch it.

So I should lovingly see everything I have created in myself. Do I need to search for things to see?

Honest, fire-full willingness will bring about the seeing. For example, underneath anger is expectation. You don't need to kill anything inside you. Killing is like cutting your branches, but the roots are still there and will keep making new branches. In this you're going into your roots by seeing what is underneath your anger.

So what is it that diminishes?

The created self and everything you see.

I'm beginning to see the drama in my life as a blessing because it is letting me see more into myself. I realize I have held on to the same old issues for years!

Exactly. People can spend their whole lifetime holding on to one small issue and never grow beyond that.

✦✦✦✦✦✦✦

Has human evolution been going on for eons, lifetime after lifetime?

To the human mind, there is time. Beyond the mind, there is no time. So in reality, a lifetime is every moment now. Many lifetimes can come and go in a moment.

If I awaken, will I affect my ancestors and my future offspring?

One's beingness does affect everything in life. It is the same when one is awakened. When you are not awakened, you give your patterns to your children and grandchildren. So of course in the awakened state there are no patterns to pass on, but everything is still being affected. But each person is being awakened for his or her *own self* entirely.

If I break a pattern in this lifetime, am I free of it?

When you think about the next day, the next lifetime, you are being irresponsible. Be in the *now*; see your patterns *now* as if there is no other day, no other lifetime. Be in the *now*.

The Heart (The Real You)

I'm trying to grasp "being in the heart." Does this mean working with the energy inside me?

When you are used to working with energy inside of you, there is still creation in you, because that energy can present you with anything you like or want. Energy can easily give a form to anything you think is true. But you don't need to believe that, even when it is happening in you. Being less (small) means you don't hang on to what is happening within. The more you don't hang on to what is happening in your life, the more you know that everything is just a creation. Being less means you are no one; you are not even energy.

Right now taste that little bit from your heart and *be* in the heart in a very sober way, letting that energy diminish in you. Be powerless. Being powerless means you are diminishing little by little. You really do not want anything, but long to be powerless in every form you see within you.

In that lessness, it's not always about feeling good. In facing the reality, you're facing everything *as is*. That does not mean only good or only happy. It can tear your heart apart, but that's okay. This little bit of realness takes daring to be able to be in the discomfort. When you taste a little bit of realness, regardless of the taste, long for that realness and never be satisfied with anything else. Reality is always heartbreaking because you've been in those beliefs a long time. In reality you always see how much unreality there is sitting in you that you thought was your own.

I'm still having a problem understanding "with the heart"; could you explain more please?

It's not like you can be with your heart by understanding with your mind. Everyone wants to understand through the mind, but it's done with the heart. The mind will pull you again and again away from your

50

heart, so keep bringing yourself back to the heart (to the real self) and putting attention on the chest area. Being awake is very different from what you currently live in and live for. You don't need to find inner satisfaction; you need to awaken. Everything you have on the surface and just below the surface, you understand. But this walk is about *not* understanding. But you can trust and you can follow. You can do that.

When we are being in our heart, is that the same thing as our inner voice or intuition?

When you are being in your heart, you'll face everything in you, but you'll face it directly. It's not an inner voice; that is your perception, because with internal dialogue you're still indirect. Instead, it's a knowing. That knowing is very subtle. Little by little you learn how to connect with your knowing. That knowing does not mean you can see it all right away. You will be shown as much as you can tolerate. Just learn to open your doors so you can be okay in the pain. In the beginning you know very little. Perceptions are much more visible inside of you. Perceptions can be honest, and they can be dishonest. So don't put all your trust in perceptions.

I'm noticing that when I'm not trying to understand all this with my mind, and I am listening more with my heart, it seems that it's going in on another level and I don't have to understand, and that feels so right.

When you have a shattering of the created self, you don't have to understand with the mind, because your heart gets it. Your heart says *yes*, but the mind doesn't trust this. Your mind doesn't want you to go this way. You don't have to understand anything; just let it be recognized by the heart, and let the shattering happen gracefully. Many people practice letting go as a spiritual practice. That never works. That's spiritual drama. People think they're letting go, and they feel superior to others. This is a twisted dishonesty.

So is being with the heart the same as staying present?

You don't need to work that way. Just love what you are tasting, as though you are a child with a wonderful piece of candy who doesn't care if you fall and hurt yourself because the candy is *so* wonderful. Wherever you see the love, just be that love. Don't worry that you're not staying present. That doesn't matter. Your love will do. What you are tasting is not a small thing, and you will always be hungry for more; so when it's available, just go for it. This is the easiest way to enter and to celebrate!

How do you take something that is unpleasant to your mind into your heart?

Delightfully. When a person labels anything as being not nice, bad, or hurtful, he or she makes it bigger. The bigger the label, the harder it is to swallow. So learn to remove the labels, and delightfully embrace. Everything is embraceable. It's you who is so used to labeling "This is not nice; this is not for me." This way you create a wall, and you don't know that this wall is built against yourself. Every wall needs to be removed by embracing delightfully. Although the taste may not be nice, that doesn't mean it's not possible for you to embrace it. Be okay with the taste, and let it come inside of you. Anything that is distasteful to you is created by you and not by another person or situation. Other people and situations are only showing you your own weakness. (The way people react to any situation comes solely from them and not from others.)

How do I move forward as I see my weaknesses and move more into the heart?

By being in the weakness all the time. That in itself determines what the next step will be for you. Seeing a glimpse of the weakness is not enough. Being in it will show you where you are. And in that, you will fall many times. Recognizing the weakness yields a different taste than being in the weakness. Shame, disappointment, and being disheartened happens in true beingness. It is not about what the mind grabs and understands. You are much more than that.

With every step you need guidance from a true teacher, because though it may sound easy, walking can be difficult. In the walking you are aware of every step, of every little corner of yourself. Being aware of every corner is a huge responsibility. Now you have no one to throw your responsibilities onto but yourself. You can't choose to stay asleep any longer. That is how you earn more awareness within. As you earn more awareness, your inner eyes are opening up little by little. You'll see parts you've never been aware of before.

When you have honest willingness, you will move through all of your discomforts regardless of what you lose. That's why every person faces his or her complete picture very differently. All bad news at the surface is good news to the innermost, because that is the time you can see most of what you're lacking. That way the picture you have about yourself gets smashed and the picture you don't want to see or believe appears. Learn to embrace that picture you have. You don't want anything in this; just offer everything you have in you. That's why you need a heart to walk.

❧❧❧❧

Some days I work twelve hours a day. I don't seem to have time to be in my heart.

You have many moments all day long when you are able to come back into your heart. Many seconds even. If you complain about not having enough time, then you are giving energy to the notion of there being not enough time. Instead, celebrate each second that you remember to come back within your heart. Putting your attention on the heart area in your chest will bring you back to the real you. Then those seconds can grow to minutes even in the midst of busyness. Let go of focusing so much on the doing; just be in your heart.

❧❧❧❧

I feel like something wants to open up inside but there is some sort of block inside of me. I want that beautiful heart connection I had after my last connection with you.

When you live for what you know is truth, then you don't make anything yours—not the beautiful feelings and not the terrible feelings. Go beyond what you think is good and bad by embracing both equally.

I feel like I'm trying to do my best, and it feels like a struggle, and sometimes I feel I'm lost.

When you are *trying to do* your best, it's like you want something. Your family, friends, and employer want you to be a certain way, and you're trying to give them what they want. But when people around you change, then you're going to fall. So don't live for others; live for *you*. That is the best way to be *with* family and friends and work. You are tearing yourself apart with the trying, and you're not fair with yourself. You need to be kind to yourself. When you are trying to be kind to others, you will always lose too much energy, and at the same time, you are being unkind toward yourself. Completely learn to live for you in an honest, fair, and kind way. Living for others won't take you anywhere. Right now it feels like you don't know where to start. Just long for that and want that. Then take a baby step to begin to live for you, and then learn to stand in that, and then take another baby step, and then learn to stand in that one. Change little by little. You decide for you.

❦❦❦❦❦

Every morning I wake up depressed because all I care about is merging with God and experiencing truth. I don't really know how to be in my heart with this longing I have.

Your longing is right, but with your longing there is a cost. Even in your longing, you still have a belief about God. Everywhere you go and in everything you are doing, you are in want of something; you're looking for something, but you're not getting it. You feel depressed, but it is not something you are going to *get*, because you already *are* that. You need to see your belief system about spirituality and allow that belief to get shattered. Come back inside and see your wants and needs about this. This is the right place to come where you can allow yourself to be shattered.

You're not going to feel good about shattering. Sometimes awakening is worse than depression. Step up, regardless of how you feel. Keep coming to these meetings, and allow yourself to be softened first instead of wanting something. In the softening you are able to absorb a little bit. Wanting makes you harder and harder. The path that you have been walking has no food for you. Even when you think, "I have no interest in the world," that doesn't mean anything. The created self is in you. So, little by little, allow yourself to soften, and in your depression, stay awake. With depression, you are taken into a deeper sleep because you don't want to face the reality of your created self. If you don't feel good, don't feel good. It's okay. This awakening and this opening is going to be different from what you have perceived or believed in the past. It's going to be very different from that.

I just can't stop weeping today, and I don't really know why.

This is so lovely to see everyone crying. It's so good to be crying, to be so comfortable in it. Being within, you learn that your beingness also has ears and eyes; everything is there. Beingness is the beginning. When you are in beingness, you begin to see from your dark room, because even if the room is dark, you can begin to see what you are holding inside you. Be in the sadness. That in itself is your invitation. Instead of keeping it secret, allow it to open up in you and be in you.

For me, I feel that everyone is my child as I do this work, and with my children I am very carefree. It's the children's job to stay with the mother, and the mother is very carefree. She does everything without any hands.

I had a longing for God that used to be very intense. It seems less now. Is there anything I can do to intensify my longing in my heart again?

The space you were in before has changed. You are changing now because of your longing; otherwise, you wouldn't allow yourself to be changed. You don't feel the same intensity, and that's okay, as long as you don't satisfy yourself in the space you are in now. You are longing for what is coming next; you want to be pure now.

❦❦❦❦

Even though I see clearly at times, I still find myself reacting with anger, and then later I soften and go back into my heart, but I'm still reacting in ways I don't like.

Because you are very much in your heart, you don't need to see yourself as two separate things; here is my created self and over there is my heart. When you stay kind with your person, you will slowly diminish in that separation, and you will be able to see clearly, and then you won't react so quickly. This way you won't allow any issue to make you reactive. In your separation, you label some parts of you as not good, and then those parts become the enemy, and then that enemy puts you down. Stay with those parts in a kind way, and stop labeling and judging them. You may have confusion in the beginning, but in time you will have clarity, and gradually that gap melts.

First you react, and then you feel guilty. Reaction and guilt go together well. Those two things feed each other. Go underneath your reaction, go underneath your anger, and instead of continuing to react, go underneath to see the cause. You will see that the cause is "I want it *my* way," so stay in the *my way* and don't feed it. Now, this will bring discomfort. So be in the discomfort, because you have no choice but to stay with the discomfort.

Why would I want to be in discomfort if it weren't presenting itself, especially if I didn't feel discomfort?

Because you are trying to keep something inside covered up. You want to keep the lid on it because you know you are going to have to face your own reality. When the lid is on, you think, "I don't want to face that," and you pretend that it's not there. But underneath, it *is* there. If you take the lid off and *be* with what is there and ask yourself, "What am I afraid of losing?" then if you see fear, you will lose the fear, and then you won't need to keep this lid tight anymore. Little tiny glimpses will keep showing you what you have put the lid on.

I'm talking about big pain, though. Why would I want to delve into that when I'm not in big pain right now?

Because you are saying that it's not there. But it *is* there, and secretly you don't want to see this part. Everything is big when you open it up; even the little pattern is big. In reality everything is big, even when we think and say, "Oh, it's just a minor thing." That's big too. No matter how much we keep the lid on, when we begin to open it up, we see it's really like a huge can of worms or a semitruck load, and it can be so much that it's hard to handle. Open it up and take the lid off by seeing who you are honestly so you can be free.

❧❧❧❧❧

Could you tell us how to like and enjoy being alone?

Make *effort* to like being alone. At first it doesn't feel good to be alone, but learning to like being alone is stepping into aloneness.

Why do I avoid being alone?

Because you don't want to accept being alone and you don't embrace your own aloneness. You don't need to feel good, but you do need to begin to embrace aloneness. Slowly you can go into greater aloneness instead of judging and running from it. Being alone is good, not bad. Begin to be with it; begin to move even further into aloneness. People try to hang on to what is at the surface: family, friends, and whatever else they might take support in as a way to avoid feeling alone. But aloneness is still there. Go back into aloneness and turn back into the real you. Aloneness is inviting you to embrace the aloneness, not move away from it. Aloneness has its grip, and you are trying to get out of it. When you feel lonely, instead of making yourself busy or phoning others, why don't you just go within and stay in the aloneness? When a person runs away from something, it makes it very big and complicated. Instead be with it in a restful way.

Honesty

I don't want to see my dishonesty. I often avoid looking for it.

One needs to be ready to bear the heartbreak of seeing. The first step is learning to see and to recognize your dishonesty. Recognize your beliefs, patterns, and desires. As you become willing to recognize everything inside of you, everything will come.

I believed that I was very honest when I was dealing with the outside world, but now I am seeing that I have been tricking myself.

Most people believe that they are being honest. But *this* is about *inner* honesty. You have your own tricks that don't let you see the ways in which you become dishonest with yourself. We *think* we are being kind and honest with others, so we believe that we are honest people. We don't think we need to be *more* honest; we tell ourselves this is good enough. This is you satisfying yourself on that surface level. But this is *not* it. The surface level is not going to satisfy you, because that surface level is going to diminish one day, and then you will end up with nothing.

So what is deeper in you? You need to dig for that. Long for that instead of satisfying yourself at the surface, because surface satisfaction is always temporary. Underneath, everybody has hidden wounds and hidden dishonesty.

Is this honesty available to us all the time, and if so, by what means can we access this?

First of all, you are born from it, and it is you who is covering up that reality.

So how do I uncover my truth? Is it through my desire, my longing for it?

First you must be dissatisfied with what you are at the surface. That dissatisfaction is a little crack in you that is the invitation to enter within. Seeing the shallowness of the surface world will show you how you can dig deeper into those beliefs, wants, needs, and patterns that have been driving you.

So this dissatisfaction comes about through anxieties, sorrows, and conflicts?

The person can be satisfied in anything, even with sorrows, but this is more of an ache that you don't understand. It is an ache that won't let you rest and pulls you. It is that little crack that makes you want to ease that thirst in any way that you can.

Sometimes in this walk I don't understand if I'm really being honest or even how to be honest.

Honesty and dishonesty cannot be understood with the mind. As you let yourself land, even in confusion, that landing itself is honesty. Being honest means you're seeing your dishonesty clearly. At the same time you see the dishonesty, your created self wants to stop you from seeing this. This too is dishonesty. So when you are seeing that you have a habit, you think, "Oh, now I get it." But when you think you've *got it*, that too is being dishonest. Don't close the door to being dishonest, and then slowly you will come to not mind that you are being dishonest.

❧❦❧❦❧❦❧

How do I become honest in seeing what's under my desires, and how do I get rid of my desires?

Recognize what is underneath your desires. Recognize how they're driving you. Instead of trying to get rid of your desires, recognize everything about them in a direct way. The more you try to get rid of desires, the more they will feel threatened and fight you. Kindly see what is underneath them. Do this not for any kind of self-gain, but because it's true for you to see. If there is any kind of self-gain, it will provide a little bit of relief, but then you will secretly go back into the same rut. See your own secrets that are driving you. Don't give a direct challenge to anything within you. Just kindly long to live the *true way*, and then slowly your desires will become powerless. Long to live honestly, regardless of what you lose.

I am trying to be honest in my interactions with others, but I get really angry with people when they don't accept my standing straight in myself and my self-honesty.

This is everyone's problem. When others have a reaction to your self-honesty, you are tempted to go back to pleasing others. You will have to be true to yourself no matter what it's costing you outside. When you see the anger in you, see what is underneath that anger. When you are expecting something from others, or from yourself, and you don't get it, you will be angry. It's *you* who is expecting. You are expecting from them and yourself too. When you don't expect anything from yourself or anything from others, there is no anger or disappointment.

❦❧❦❧❦❧❦

Let's just say that I think I don't have any more attachments regarding a particular issue, but how will I really know that I've completely melted in it?

In every action or reaction, you have to look to see if you are becoming big. You may start improving, and of course you will, but that triggers the ego: "Oh, I'm growing deeper and unattached." Keep your head down; stay small.

If I don't have any attachment to events in my life, is that simplicity?

Detachment from your experiences is not simplicity. Simplicity is when you are just seeing and experiencing your attachments, not trying to fix them or detach from them. So *see* that you are attached; *see* that you are touching the truth of an attachment that is happening, and see that it is true. But trying to be detached from your experience only closes the door.

You don't need to define simplicity; simplicity just comes and fills you. Recognize when simplicity comes; let go of looking for simplicity. Detachment happens within. It is not like you can try to be detached. You still have hidden agendas. You can disconnect from a person and let him or her go, but you still have to deal with you. Just deal with your own attachments and you will become detached; it will just happen. The key is honesty within.

✺✺✺✺✺✺✺

Sometimes I'm unsure of what I'm feeling, whether it is love, sadness, peace, or happiness. How do I stay honest with this confusion?

Really open up within yourself regarding everything you feel; whether it is love or sadness, just stay with it. It's okay. Then you will continue to move within.

Sometimes I feel there's almost a magnetic pull toward another person's heart. Is that pull into another's heart something to be avoided?

When you are honest with yourself and gentle with yourself, you are automatically more honest and gentle with others. So if you want to be more present with others, stay within. Anything you see outside of you is also about you. Bring it into you.

How can I be better at recognizing what is coming from my feelings and emotions and what is coming from my heart?

At first feelings and emotions are strong, simply because they *are* tangible. Just recognize your feelings and emotions. Recognizing this is good. Being in the recognition is part of opening up and entering closer to the heart. Entering the heart is seeing your layers. You have had only little glimpses of your heart because your beliefs, patterns, etc., stand in the way. Acknowledge all the emotions and just be with them. That will take you to your heart. You can't do it quickly; it takes time.

But am I just participating with these emotions, or am I really seeing them and trying to be with them? How do I know I am honest in this?

You become completely blind in anything you are participating in, but others can see it in you. You have softness that is allowing you to see. Because of your softness, you are able to stay in the pain that arises; just keep going through the layers.

What if the feeling is love?

Recognize what emotions are in the love. That itself will show you. *Feeling* love is different from real love, which carries no feelings, no emotions. It is formless.

෴෴෴෴

When you're a child, you have an honest intimacy with everything. Children seem to be naturally in the heart. How and why do we lose this?

The child recognizes its innocence. But the child doesn't know how to live from that place of innocence and still be able to get along in the world. So as children grow up, they get bent by the created world. The innocence has not gone anywhere. But the outside world becomes more and more embedded within us because we are shown and taught that we should live a certain way. With this walk, we are learning how to live in that innocence again in a pure way, a true way, without letting our real self be buried under surface things.

Hope

I want so much to meet God. I hope that I am coming closer to experiencing that.

Hope is not real. Hoping to live a different way, hoping to see God—that's unreal. In reality there is no hope. Hope is a created idea. It's like you are hoping for some miracle. You see that you are in pain, and you are hoping to be pain-free in the future. When you continue to hope, you don't look inside for what has been pressed down within you. Be hopeless. It's not a good feeling, but in reality it's good.

Will hopelessness threaten the person?

It will if you make it that way. There is sadness in you when you say "I have no hope." It is really good to be in that sadness, because then you start going deeper. The sadness is a second step, and many are tempted to run away from that. But stay in that sadness.

You have to stay so kind and gentle and simply switch your attention toward a pattern. But when you say "Okay, I'm going to work on that!" you threaten the pattern and it is hidden again. So be okay with seeing the pattern. Once you see it, you know it's okay to be in it. When you're okay to be in it, then the pattern starts opening up. Your inner eye starts opening up, and you see that "Oh, it's all about me; it's all about what I have created."

Don't threaten your person. Just simply see and enter by keeping your face toward your patterns. Patterns are tricky. You only see the pattern through an issue, and as soon as the issue in front of you is gone, you close the door to the pattern also. And now you don't know *how* to look or *where* to look. Just keep a little thread of the pattern, keeping your face at all times toward the pattern in order to come closer to that pattern. That way it will slowly show itself.

Everyone's fantasy is, "Okay, now I'll go meet God; now I'll have self-realization." It's not like that. Everyone's thoughts and ideas about these beliefs need to shatter. Discover *you*. Being unfolded is the very beginning of awakening. In continuing to discover yourself, you will see you are the one who has created everything, and as you see this, little by little, everything will melt.

You say hope is unrealness, but sometimes it is helpful, isn't it? I come here to the meetings with a hope that I'll learn something from you that will improve me.

Why don't you come just for the love? Your heart is pulling you to love. You will be frustrated if you hope. With heart love you won't have any internal dialogue. Your heart *is* pulling you, but your mind says it wants to learn more.

Fear

Let's say a person has her life earnings in a savings account and she has a fear that she might lose all her money if the economy is bad, but at the same time these savings give her peace of mind. Is that leaning?

I'll tell you first of all that, no, that is not peace of mind. What the person has created is fear of losing those savings. First comes ownership and possessiveness. Then fear comes that she won't have enough so she needs to save. With that belief, all sorts of anxiety is born, and the person doesn't even want to think about losing. People think they feel good when they have savings, and they feel bad when they don't.

It's not about saving or not saving; it's about the fear of not having. People need to see that. Go back in the fear where you are afraid of losing. Don't turn your face from it. Do this little by little, but not all at once. Take tiny steps to where you become okay to lose. Cut all your stories short and come back into yourself; otherwise, stories just get more and more sophisticated. Take a shortcut to yourself by cutting the long stories short. Choose to cut your story short and come back.

❦❦❦❦❦❦

I would like to ask more about experiencing and releasing fears. Is it possible to think your way into a fear even when you aren't experiencing fear?

Yes. You just ask for fear, and it will come up sooner or later. It's your honest willingness that opens you up. Stay in it as it comes up, little by little.

I realize that I am in fear a lot of the time.

Yes. For example, think of the out-of-control fear a person might experience on a crashing plane. All of us are that afraid all the time. This is just one instance when it becomes apparent. The willingness comes whenever a person says, "I'm going to dive into this fear that I keep pushing away." See the fear clearly. See on a deep level what you are afraid of losing. Stay with it as it gets more uncomfortable; stay with the fear as your story unfolds. If you are able to honestly see your fears and become aware of what you are afraid of losing, then you are willing. But you have to be willing to stay with it, sometimes for a long time.

Is fear something that we project into the future, or is it more of a belief system?

Fear is everything. It is both a projection and a belief. Always ask yourself, "What am I afraid of losing?" Often people think, "If I think it is going to happen, then I am going to make it a reality and manifest what I am afraid will happen." Actually it's the opposite. Let yourself go into the fear completely. For example, a person is afraid of dying in a plane crash and losing his body. If he would stay in that fear until he could be completely with the shattering of his body, he would then lose that fear. But it is difficult. Typically we see the fear of death a little bit, experience what that would be like a little bit, and then we say, "That's enough; okay, I got it!" You need to really go into the core of it and the absolute depths of it, where you see the whole family of fears surrounding death. Do this with whatever fear you're working with.

So if the same fear comes up over and over again, then we haven't cleared it.

Yes, because we are not truly *being* in it. Being *in* fear at first is like stepping into a dark room that you are completely unfamiliar with. First you are afraid to step into it because you don't know what's there. So step in from your side. Do this little by little, but don't step back out; continue to step forward into it. Continue to lose what you are afraid of losing, willingly, by giving preference to honesty. Keep losing it, and stay in that losing state.

Sometimes I feel deeply afraid for no reason. What could you tell me about that?

Even when you don't have a clue why you are afraid, stay with it, and stay open to see it. That will open it up in you. Instead of trying to figure it out, just *be* with the fear and be open to it. It's good to be curious and to like to see. Curiosity can take you to the deepest.

I saw a man being murdered when I was a child. I feel I still carry that man's pain with me. I have a lot of fear surrounding this.

First be in the clarity about what the fear is about. You are carrying an accumulation of many judgments about what you saw.

But this was a real event!

Real or not real, you are only able to see when you take the direct pain into you. You can only be direct with it by releasing your judgments: "Those people were bad." Then you carry this with you in a box all your life. That carrying does not serve any justice for them, the victim, or yourself. See that and let it open up in you. You don't have to judge others or the murderers; just take the pain directly into you. Let the pain open you up to see you.

How can I let this open me up?

Allow the direct pain.

Can this total shattering happen in an instant?

Are you able to take it in an instant? You cannot take it in an instant. It comes little by little. You may want that for yourself and say, "I want to get it over with all at once," but it has to be little by little.

Well, I feel this is all happening so fast that it's scary. So what can I do?

Anything that is happening is happening because you are allowing it. If it is happening, just give it permission. Just sink in it. It's okay.

I've been walking this path for two years, and I see myself approaching the emptiness that used to scare me. Now I'm enjoying this, and at the same time I'm scared that it might go away and l will be back to the way I used to be.

Then stay with that. See it as another thing that you want and, as with anything you want, you will become a prisoner of it. You don't need anything. Let emptiness come, and then land in the emptiness. You don't need to hold on to the emptiness. Everything that you land in, you'll see more and you will move forward by seeing more dishonesty. You are landing in your perceptions, but you are still not landing in your heart. You are still outside of yourself, and you need to come inside. Most people earn some amount of energy. With that energy, you feel everything, and you will feel the emptiness, but it's still outside of you. Everything needs to land in you in order to be the *true way* of being.

✍❀✍❀✍❀✍❀

I've had some bad experiences in the past, and I keep reliving them. I have a fear that I might have to encounter them again, but the harder I try to let them go, the stronger they become.

That never works. Maybe a person who wants to let go of something will get temporary relief: "Okay, I did let go, and I'm okay now." But you cannot let go of anything. *See* that you're not letting go, that you're still holding on to the memories. Just *be* in it in an honest way. That is letting go, and when it happens, you become more awakened. When the fear comes, open your heart and open your arms; let it happen in you. Let it do whatever it wants to do to you, fearlessly. Face it instead of paralyzing yourself in the fear.

I have a fear of dying and losing my body.

Actually, the bigger fear is losing the identity, not losing the body. Losing the identity is like being thrown from the sky.

✍❀✍❀✍❀✍❀

It's liberating to feel no fear, to trust you so much, and to just let this be what it is, even when painful.

Being in means continuing to stay in awareness even when it is emotionally painful. But the created self doesn't want to be in pain too long. When you find yourself moving away from your heart pain, you can use that as a way to remind yourself to come back into yourself again and again. In doing this, you're learning to be honest with your pain. It's liberating because now you don't have to run away from it. This is a new way of being. It is a bit challenging to learn to be in the pain all the time. Just learn to be in the pain little by little, in a new way.

I now see that it's nothing but fear.

Face the full loss in you intensely. Go to the full intensity with it, and then it will melt. Rather than protecting yourself from the fear, let it land in you. Here is an example: Someone is afraid of losing his sister because she is ill and she may die. This person needs to sit with that fear until it takes him all the way to the end—where he *has* lost his sister, where she is dead. Then there is no more hope and the person will simply have to start accepting her death; then the fear will lose its power.

Illness and Pain

Is physical pain destined?

The concept regarding destiny is a belief. Whatever you believe, you will make that belief real for yourself. But that doesn't mean there is any reality in it. You say to yourself, "This physical pain is my destiny; *I need* to be in this pain because this pain is not going away." But there is no truth in this belief. You make this belief real, and because you believe, or are trying to believe, that maybe this is destiny, you give power to this. Instead, try *being,* in a direct way, in the physical pain. Direct beingness helps you to be in the pain. You're looking for some answers. You don't need any answers. Little by little, stay in the pain. You can't understand what I'm saying right away; you won't get it right away. Belief systems won't let us have a direct relationship with anything; they stay in between.

Being with the pain is having a direct relationship with it. You won't get it in a thinking way. Let it happen in a direct way that bypasses everything—the mental and the emotional. That's what the meetings and sessions are for. The meetings let you be in the directness with yourself—not in the thinking, not in the beliefs, and not in the ways you are living in among society. If you're standing in your own self, then nothing bends you.

Your weakness is that you don't know your own ground. Finding your own ground comes in a direct way, not in a mental way. Everything is easy to understand in a mental way because it's a familiar way of this world. That's why I'm speaking so simply—because it's hard for the person to *get it*; because it's unfamiliar, unexpected. Believing is easy, but this directness seems difficult because the belief system is in the foreground; the belief system is already in the way.

I am experiencing a lot of back pain. I am aware of it, but it seems far away and I'm not being in it. Can you help me to understand how to be in this pain?

This is showing you how you are distancing yourself. You are being distant from the discomfort. Look at it this way: the back pain is helping you, and through this pain you are able to say that you are aware of the pain being far away. See the distancing and the desire for the pain to disappear. The pain is in you. You have to be the one in it. Look for what is in the back pain that you fear. That will help you come closer to what beliefs and fears you have about this pain.

So are you saying I can't treat the pain?

No, that is a surface issue; the way you choose to treat the pain is up to you. Your question for me is how to *be* in the pain, which happens at deeper levels. If you treat the pain and lose your ability to focus or to be in it, then you know you are really distancing yourself from it. You are hanging out at the surface and cannot be with yourself.

I see how I have made myself a victim of my own patterns, but I know my pain is not an enemy.

Yes. People always think that they need to protect themselves. But it is the opposite. Open your doors and let in whatever comes to you. The enemy is the protecting. It is a dishonesty to think, "I'm going to get over this pain." Don't think that way; allow the pain to be a guest. A good and loving host will never ask his or her guest to leave. If the guest is in your home and feels welcome there, then one day you and the guest will become as one. If you truly think that the pain doesn't need to go, then one day there will be no separation. It's the same thing with love. You become love; you become pain. Others see it in you, but you don't see it so clearly in yourself because you're becoming that. You can see it in others, though. You have to trust that you know how true it is within you. This is the *true way* of being. Open more of you in order to be more with the pain in you. Be one with everything all of the time.

I'm struggling with restlessness, lack of sleep, and various illnesses. How do I deal with these illnesses?

Try not to get rid of them or run away from them. Little by little, learn to be in them with acceptance, warmly. Even the physical challenges, the illnesses, are not worth running away from; it's worth being in them along with the restlessness. Be aware that you are experiencing the restlessness so you can be in it. By being in it, you learn little by little. These challenges don't come up only once, so bring everything you have and be willing to be in those challenges warmheartedly and be okay little by little, in a restful way.

Running away from or hoping you'll get rid of these challenges is called dishonesty. Stay honest forever, regardless of the challenges. Choose to stay honest regardless of the cost. You might feel that it's not right, but even if you have those feelings, respect those feelings and at the same time stay with your honesty. The bigger the challenge, the more it's worth being in. As the challenge extends, increase your awareness as well. Stay with what you are moving through.

What you are familiar with does not like it when you choose to be in what is unfamiliar. It's as if you are taking away the food from that familiar, unwell part of yourself. The truth does not choose anything, but it always feels that way as long as there are untrue parts alive in you. Recognize this, and when you are recognizing, know that you do not need to run away from the unfamiliar no matter how strange the discomfort feels.

I notice I need more sleep; I am very tired lately. My work used to energize me; now it tires me. Is this because I'm trying to be more aware of myself?

As you walk, you will experience many things. These experiences are completely opposite of what you usually expect from a spiritual walk, because this is not about *getting* something. It's not about *being* somebody. It's about the truth. Standing in the little bit of honesty that you now have is giving you more awareness about yourself. Whichever way you are aware of yourself, learn to be in it. You need to be in every part of yourself. If something is driving you, it means it's outside of you. Knowing that, open yourself up more so you can be in what is driving you.

ᢍᡃᢍᡃᢍᡃᢍᡃ

When I am with my pain I can get lost in the drama of it.

People invest much of themselves in the drama of pain. And when they decide to come back into their heart and *be* with that pain, it creates a worse pain and intensifies the thoughts and inner dialogue about it. Lots of people do experience this. But once they know that this is just mental dialogue that they don't need to listen to, they can come back into the heart knowing that there is no truth in the dialogue. The dialogue and thoughts will slowly diminish. Recognize those inner thoughts and fears about your pain as a habit, and then you can take the authority away from them. The thoughts will try to make you think you're going in the wrong direction, but trust coming back into you. Even when the thoughts about your pain get loud, just continue to come back into you. Bring your physical and emotional attention to *now* and into your heart, because it takes a long, long time to quiet the mind. Keep coming back into your heart.

Patterns

You tell us to stay in our patterns. What is the definition of a pattern? Certain things are very obviously patterns, but others can be tricky.

Yes, patterns can be tricky because the person is already interwoven into them. For example, many times we briefly realize, "This is how I am often exposed or hurt," but it's only momentary. The more difficult thing to say is, "I would really like to be in that pattern now." By doing that, you will see things in glimpses. It's not like we get the whole picture all at once. This is partly because we are woven into our patterns (willful, stubborn, critical, idealistic, cheerful, prideful, gluttonous, etc.) and can't see them, and partly because it is very threatening to the created self. This path is not for everyone, because not everyone is willing to go through that pain.

Seeing is very valuable. It is a precious thing to begin to see and to keep seeing more and more. But it's not necessary to label anything a pattern. Perhaps you respond angrily to something and you begin to see how often that happens to you. Deal with that first; there is no need to label it as a pattern.

⨀❧⨀❧⨀❧⨀

I have followed a guru for many years, and I have given and done much for others. But since I have met you, I have begun to look at myself, and now I feel hopeless about all my patterns.

When you don't live for your real self, you continue to be in the created self. You get wrapped up easily and blindly. You are openhearted, but you're using that for the lower self. You suffer more than a normal person. You are not asleep, but you're being driven by your patterns.

All my patterns are huge. I cannot stay with myself even for a minute; I can't stand the discomfort.

With the same heart you have for others, use that toward seeing your pattern and not your judgment toward yourself. You don't need a way out. You just need to embrace your mess with the same heart you already have. Use that loveliness in seeing what you are like, even though the taste is bitter. Don't give power to that taste. Use your qualities so you can be in the same wonderful way with yourself. You don't need to feel sorry for yourself, even in seeing all of this mess, because that creates self-pity. In self-pity you'll look for relief, and you will say, "I can't take it anymore." You have a delightfulness that you've been using to give to others. Don't waste a second, because every moment is another chance to see these patterns in you. Be in that delightfulness, and put it toward yourself. See your patterns as though they are a little baby. You don't need to judge that baby. Just use your tenderness and your kindness to be closer to the baby. You cannot *fix* your patterns, but you *can* apply gentleness and kindness when you are in them.

✍❧✍❧✍❧

I have a very strong pattern of being willful. When I am like that, I feel really hard in my heart, and it doesn't feel right when I am in that state.

If it doesn't feel right, that's good. Learn to be in the okayness little by little even when you slip back and feel the same way again. If you continue to participate with and wrestle with the thing that doesn't feel right, then you'll never solve the problem. Decide to stop running, and no matter how it feels, stay kind. In that kindness, remember to do this little by little and be okay in it. Don't expect that the feeling will go away. That feeling does not need to go away. Learn to be okay in that feeling and trust your okayness. Take baby steps *all* the time toward being okay with seeing all of yourself. You cannot run away from yourself, and when you know that, you won't need to waste your time trying to run away. Just face it in a delightful way.

I've been noticing my tendency to celebrate my joy and be outside myself a lot. I'm learning that I don't need to celebrate outside. But this makes me sad in a lot of ways.

Now you can recognize this a little bit. Now you see that anything you're expressing outwardly takes you out of yourself. Feeling the sadness about yourself in this can really bring you so much deeper. There's a cost to you. For example, where you used to feel celebration all the time, now you're going to feel the opposite. *That* is what you need to be in. There is nothing else to do.

I repeatedly get intensely stressed if I need to take a day off work. I fear and worry and agonize about how to ask for that day off. This has been a pattern for years for me.

Just be comfortable with your own answer inside of you first. Don't go directly to your projection about what your employer might say or do. First be with your own discomfort in asking for time off. That in itself is a lot. In fretting and working yourself up, you are like a snowball rolling around, becoming bigger and bigger. So when this starts, say, "Stop it. Stop growing this anxiety. Now I'm going to be in it and see what my thoughts are and what my beliefs are about my discomfort." Your discomfort is about speaking up. Stay with that discomfort, because it will show everything about you. When you try to change yourself, you are not being authentic. First be with the discomfort and see what is in it for you.

Personal Relationships

I recently had a strong feeling of being unfairly treated, and I wanted to justify myself. I'm having trouble letting go of the pain of this inside me.

This incident is showing you how you protect yourself from pain, embarrassment, and feeling disheartened. Continue to go back into what you remember of the incident until you allow the whole event to enter you. Then, slowly, you will learn to feel it and to let yourself feel the pain. It's okay. What you are being shown is valuable, so don't turn your face from it. Letting it inside will unfold many things in you.

If others are in pain or suffering in some way, I try to help, but then I bring their pain home. I agonize over it.

Learn how to *be* in your identification of this attachment. It's not that you are going to fix your attachment, because you won't be able to let go of your attachment; you cannot do it. But you *can* see it first. Learn how to be very honest in the attachment. Learn to be in that true place where you don't touch it and you just let it happen. Let it open you up. That opening up in you is so beautiful. You won't think about others anymore because you will begin to see your own beauty differently. In the attachment, it doesn't initially feel beautiful. In the beginning it feels like something is being torn apart inside you. It's not a good feeling, but stay in it and don't worry about how you're feeling; just give priority to what is true for you to be. If you give preference to truth even though it doesn't necessarily give you pleasant feelings, you will be able to grow within, and then you can be you.

I want to help others, but I also realize I'm letting others bend me away from my walk.

You are seeing that you are bending in your weakness and you don't know how to stand firm in your own truth. If you are outward, you will keep bringing all the pain and anxiety back with you and into you. No one can do anything for others, but you can be *you*. That is possible in you. Learn about yourself through everything you do. It's not about others. Bring awareness continually forward in you all the time. Remember, it's not about fixing yourself.

✣✣✣✣✣✣

I am very concerned about dealing with my family's demands and at the same time trying to do this walk.

Even though you know what this walk means, you are postponing dealing with it. When you know that this is in the way, stay in that issue, because it matters. Even if you think it's a little thing, keep focusing on your family. The family is already within you; come back into you and be in that issue that is blocking you. From there you are able to see your feelings and your emotions. When you go outward into your family, you cannot see you. You only see the family. You don't need to lose you. You say that it is too uncomfortable—that there is too much pain—so you busy yourself in others again. But your responsibility is to stay in that blockage.

I'm also having trouble with my husband.

It's not about him. If you are suffering, it's about you. You can't fix him, right? There is always the hope that maybe one day you will fix him, but it won't matter. Even if you *do* fix him, it won't make a difference in you or for you. The most important thing that he is showing you is what you need to see in yourself.

So he is the way he is because of m;, it's my fault?

It's not your fault; it's a weakness. It's an attachment, and attachments blind you. So try to see the attachment and then be *in* the attachment, and slowly you can unfold that attachment. This is possible for you to do.

How would I do that?

That's what these meetings are for. The meetings are to learn hc
unfold, learn how to be with what you are currently in. You untoia
step-by-step, and as you grow, you are freed from your created self and
its attachments (such as wanting to fix him or change anything from
the outside). If you are free from it, then you are okay. Whichever way
he is, is *his* choice.

So, in other words, you're saying, "Let go."

That "letting go" does happen. But before it really happens, you are in
the attachment or are *trying* to let go of the attachment, and because
of that it doesn't happen. Mentally you are telling yourself, "Okay, I'm
letting go; it's not in my hands anymore." But inside you, that attachment
is still there. You're still wishing, secretly, that you could help him or
change him, or maybe he *is* changing, but that won't enable you to let
go. Be with your attachment first.

ぶ❀ぶ❀ぶ❀ぶ❀

*Lately I am being true to myself and I wish to withdraw from others, but
people don't understand or they misunderstand.*

Yes, people can feel threatened by this, and this can bend you away
from yourself. That is okay; you don't need to worry about what they're
thinking, just stay honest about who you are. Everyone is playing a
game, and you are playing according to what they want you to be, and
when you decide to change the rules for yourself, they don't like it. If
you can stand straight in being what you are, that can help others too.
Even when they're reacting, standing straight within will help them.
Otherwise you are just feeding other people's blindness and your own.
As you wake up, you become an example to them, and they can then
wake up too. But initially they will react because something is being
taken away from them.

ぶ❀ぶ❀ぶ❀ぶ❀

When an issue arises in relationships, is it be best to work out that issue together or spend some time apart to clear it?

Whichever way you choose is okay as long as you do know it's all you. Your partner is showing you something about *you*. When you direct the arrow of this awareness toward yourself, letting it land inside you, this will create enough space. It is only when you don't let your arrow land in you that you feel choked and then you think you need space. There is nothing wrong with staying or going to resolve an issue, as long as you are honest with yourself. You feel choked when you don't give that issue enough room in you.

Sometimes I feel that when I go off alone, clarity comes quicker, but then there seems to be a separation in the partnership.

Just remember that the issues are in you. The partner is just showing you by poking you. Understand that you don't know how to lie with those issues in *you*.

What do you mean by "lie"?

A pattern in you is being shown to you by your partner, and you don't like that pattern in you. So you say, "I don't like that," and a war begins inside of you. Now you feel as if you need to be alone. You feel you need lots of space in this war. If you warmly embrace what you are experiencing within your patterns—taking space or working it out together—it doesn't matter.

If you or your partner separate from each other, you may feel relieved for the moment. You think you're okay now, but that pattern can still be hidden in you. Discomfort does increase when something is being triggered by your partner, because it's so close and you don't have room to run away from your own pattern. When you learn to embrace your own patterns, and you are kind with them, you won't scare them. Love to see, long to see, and always stay open to see *you*.

In my relationships I sometimes don't want to connect with my partner because I don't like what I see. I have an aversion to what I see in other people sometimes.

You're still very indirect with yourself. You pick something wrong, something little at first, in all your relationships. Learn to be very direct with yourself about that. If you're not direct with yourself, you'll continue to create more indirectness. Stay direct even when it hurts.

What do you mean by "direct"?

The way you are speaking right now, you're indirect with yourself. You are not letting yourself feel anything.

So you mean go right to the heart of what is there when I'm speaking?

Yes. That does not mean you should fix the way you speak; it is showing you that the way you speak is indirect. In indirectness there is protection. This protection means you're working too hard to make everything work in your marriage. It's the same in everything you do. The first thing to do is let yourself feel, and if you let yourself feel, you will let things come closer to you, and then you're able to feel your disheartened feelings. You don't need to protect yourself from your disheartened feelings; just *be* in those feelings. When you're just being in the feelings, you'll be one step closer to yourself and you'll be able to see more of you. Your disheartened feelings do not need to go away; just learn to be in them in a warm way. When you know they are there, then you will learn to be in them all the time. Your disheartened feelings are making you softer.

You are saying to be in my disheartened feelings, but how do I go there?

You *are* in these disheartened feelings right now. Be in your heart, be disappointed, be in pain, and be in those disheartened feelings. Be in them so that you are able to be direct with yourself in a warm way. Trust that, and as you trust, love that little bit of trust, as it will let you go deeper. You don't need to change yourself; let the change come to you through love and trust.

My partner would like me to make more income, and I'm willing, but I also want to just be.

Don't make an issue about the income. Simply move in whichever direction you choose to make an income. When you make an issue of it, then you make a big deal of it. Then it becomes bigger than you. When it is bigger than you, you can't see you.

Yes, that is what happens. I become confused and lost in making money. Is it that I am used to seeing all this as either good or bad and having judgments?

That too. It's not only about money, which you already know. On one side you see your need for money to survive. On the other side you want to just *be*. Instead of tearing yourself apart, just let yourself move gently toward whatever you need to do at the surface. You can make a big deal and say to yourself, "I can only be on the surface" or "I can only be inside." But you can't be in both at the same time. Even when you're out in the world, you're still thinking in your mind about being inside. Nothing is good or bad in anything on the surface if you simply and effortlessly move through it.

꧁ꕥꕥꕥꕥ꧂

I feel like I'm trying to do my best in all my relationships, and it feels like a struggle, and sometimes I feel I'm lost.

When you are trying to do your best, it means you want something. Your family, friends, or your employer want you to be a certain way, and so you are trying to do your best. But when other people change, which they will, then you're going to fall. So don't live for others; live for you. That is the best way to live *with* people. You are tearing yourself apart with the trying, and you're not being fair with yourself. You need to be kind to yourself. When you try to be kind to others, you will always lose too much energy, and at the same time, you are being unkind toward yourself. Completely learn to live for *you* in an honest way, a fair way, and a kind way.

Living for others won't take you anywhere. Right now it feels like you don't know where to begin doing this. First you must decide to long for that and want that. Then, little by little, you will take a small step, and then you will learn to stand in it. Then you will take another baby step and learn to stand in that. But first, you decide for you.

It seems to me that we have been conditioned to believe that if we are living only for ourselves we are being selfish, but that if we live for others and our duties, this is morally higher.

When you live for others, you may be trying to show what a good mother you are, what a good wife you are, or what a good employee or employer you are. But when your walls drop, you already *are* everything. You don't have to prove how good you are; you just simply *are*.

But what if you truly believe you want to live for others?

That doesn't matter. It's like you're pleasing yourself with that belief. There's nothing wrong with that, but if you want to be in the purity, that belief is in the way. The desire to please others is a dishonesty.

Why were we taught by our parents, teachers, and religions that we need to do things for others and that doing things for others will bring us happiness?

You can be in the system forever, but one day you have to let it all shatter and fall down. Even though we were taught things by the people who love us the most, that doesn't mean those things are truth. Truth is your own choice, and it does cost.

You say to be kind to yourself, but sometimes being kind to oneself means being unkind to somebody else.

It *feels* that way. So many people are mistaken by this. They think, "I have to be kind to the other person so I will take the kindness away myself." You are trying to be kind, but you are serving unkindness. ___ is such a big misunderstanding. You think, "If I'm not kind, then I am untrue to the other person," but at the same time you are untrue to yourself. Over time you work harder and harder to try to be kind to others and less and less kind to yourself. Being honest is everyone's longing. Being honest takes you toward the truth. You cannot swallow the whole truth at first, because you don't have the capacity. Taking tiny steps of honesty is how you can be true to yourself.

How do I learn to love someone unconditionally?

You can't. You need to learn to love yourself first. Whenever we are learning to love another person, we can only give so much. You cannot give your whole self, because you have your own holdings (patterns) inside of you. Whatever your holdings are within you, you will give *that* to others. For example, if you have anger inside, you will automatically give your anger to others, knowingly or unknowingly.

So how do I get rid of the anger?

You see what is underneath the anger. When you love yourself by seeing through all your anger, all your fear, you *become* love. So you have to clean your own bucket.

❦❧❦❧❦❧❦

I'm having a lot of doubts and fears about doing this self-reflection and being with it all the time and still being able to be a wife and mother.

As you move inside of you, of course the doubts and fears come. That's very natural. Spouses and children show you where your flaws are. Use that to focus more within. That's how you can be better, not as a mother or wife, but you *be* you, flaws and all. Take away the role of wife and mother, and you may feel there is no one left. Whatever is left over, see *that* part in you. See it and be in it. What is there to lose?

That's a very encouraging line—"What is there to lose?"

You said that when your husband passed away, you had no guilt. Can you say more?

I learned before his death that I didn't need to interfere in his life in any way. I learned to embrace him with my whole heart, regardless of what he was or where he was coming from. I was able to love him the way he was. Usually partners are trying to change each other, which is interference. Freedom and happiness come from accepting everything about another person.

I have a problem saying no to people when they request things from me. I don't want to disappoint or anger or let down anyone else.

See what is inside of you that keeps saying yes, and ask yourself, "How is this serving me, and what am I getting out of it?" When you agree to things you don't want to do, then you live for those outer forces and for others. You are living for *their* feelings. You become completely unaware of yourself when you are only aware of other people's feelings.

First, realize your own feelings, even when you are hurt. Be in the feelings in order to see your own weakness and what is underneath that weakness. Let it unfold in you by being in it. If you aren't being in it, then you won't let it unfold, and instead you will start thinking, "Maybe this is the reason I do this or that." That can be an untrue reason.

Stay in those feelings even though you feel uncomfortable. Saying no to other people's wishes does not mean you are being selfish. It just means you are being what you *are* and at the surface it will feel as though you're being selfish. But choose the honesty that is *in* you, not what is outside of you. You cannot understand others unless you are completely true to yourself. So if you're being driven by other people's wants, needs, and feelings, you are away from yourself.

I sometimes feel used by people.

If you feel used by others, it's because of you—your own sleepiness. It is your own choice to be bent by others.

Taking a step toward acting on your own truth will bring up lots of guilt. Instead of thinking about people taking something away from you, be in the hurt and in the disappointment, and at the same time be within you all the time. By doing this, you will be able to see your own weaknesses instead of being in your scattered behavior. The scattered behavior won't let you land in you. Even though you do have good qualities, you still suffer because you don't know your own lacks in the midst of the qualities you have.

Don't bend in front of your own emotions; just recognize them. Stay in the desperation—the desperation to recognize every part of yourself. The more you recognize your parts, the more you're able to see that this is *you*.

Could you explain a bit more about how not to be a doormat while living in this world?

Being a doormat is okay. You can completely be a doormat. Your perception of being a doormat is that it is a bad way to be. But if you want to be a doormat, then it's okay to lie down on the floor and have everyone walk over you, because that is what you choose to be. However, if your focus is on pleasing other people and you try to be a doormat (or try *not* to be a doormat), either way you have lost you. The focus must always be on you. Other people are only showing you what you are lacking within. Because of your own patterns, you close the door to your own awareness.

When we are living with people, we have to deal with them all the time, so isn't it about them also?

Use those people to find ways to open up. Deal with them with openheartedness. When you start thinking, "I *have* to deal with them," you will narrow your heart and come out of your inner self, and then you begin the thinking process again. When you are *being* with an open heart, no matter what another person is doing, you are not making that person's business yours. You are letting that person be his or her own business.

I'm always trying to make sure everyone is happy. I avoid conflict, and I try to make sure no one is upset; and if there is conflict, it hurts me a lot.

You keep putting bandages one on top of the other, and one day you will have to take them off one by one. You are putting these bandages on purposely, keeping everything smooth so it won't hurt you. Who are you saving, others or you? This is a misunderstanding. You think you're doing good things for others, but really you don't want to be hurt or feel pain. When you keep the arrow on you, it will show you much more about your habit of avoiding the pain. If you are a diplomat all the time, you are knowingly creating an illusion for yourself, and then it becomes a cage.

I guess I believe that living to make others happy is a good way to live.

That's right; it's a belief, but it's not reality.

I know you keep telling us to be absolutely honest, but if I become absolutely honest with others, I won't have any friends!

How will you know what your friends' reactions will be until you *are* that direct with them? You have a belief that if you are direct with your friends, you will lose them. That's just your perception. You know that you're not serving any honesty to your friends; you know that you are just trying to please them, even when you don't want to. How can you be so dishonest with your friends?

Being honest all the time, does it work? I think people are not capable of hearing the truth.

This is the misunderstanding. Everyone thinks that way.

We are in blindness about ourselves but have no trouble seeing qualities and patterns that we don't like in others. I realize those qualities are in ourselves also. Could you say more on this subject?

Turning the arrow to the self allows your inner eye to start opening up, which then allows you to see your own patterns and weaknesses. When you awaken, you start to see the good qualities also. But first you begin to come back inside yourself and open your own doors to see your own dishonesty, your own guck, and the way everything has been pushed down inside you.

When we are feeding a relationship with dishonesty, the other person knows deep down inside. Everyone's heart knows. On the surface we don't want to be naked, and neither does the other person. When one person decides that there will be no more dishonesty in the relationship, the other person's heart responds and loves this new honesty. On the surface, the other person is used to being in the game of dishonesty, so he or she may react and be uncomfortable at first. But in reality everyone's heart longs for this honesty. We don't need to lie, and we *do* need to recognize the lie. The created self is all drama, and everyone is caught up in the drama, but it's not real. It's really so simple; just come back into you. It can be hard to come back, but that is the cost. It's a lovely cost when you find your real self.

Sometimes I feel that my obligations to my relationships are in the way of this walk. I feel real discomfort in this right now.

Just be in the discomfort. It's okay. It is wonderful to be in the discomfort that you're experiencing right now. Something is being invited in you at this moment, so just notice that there is an issue here for you about relationships. You don't need to do anything about it, and you don't need to fix it. This is being honest and direct.

It's already turning into something else. It went right through me, so simply! Is this because I was able to take it in a direct way?

Right now a shattering is happening, and because you're letting your discomfort *be* in you, you are letting the shattering happen. It's okay.

Well, this shattering is very gentle, but before it was hard, even brutal.

This is because now you're *in* you, and before you were distant from yourself. When you are distant from your real self and a shift happens, it's like a big noise. But when you come close to yourself, it is so delicate, so gentle, and so subtle. Sitting in these meetings is a huge help. It's a help that the mind does not understand.

Parenting

Can you speak a little bit about parenting young children? I want my children to have that balance of being free, being loved, and also having rules and discipline. So how can we achieve a balance?

Children show us so much about ourselves. They show us all our fear, our anxiety, our control, and our attachments. All these things become clear in being a parent. You need to see those parts in *you* first and not focus so much on the surface, wondering how you are supposed to be with your children. When you become direct with yourself, then whatever you do at the surface will become natural. When you are true to yourself, then that will bring simplicity. In the simplicity, everything is easy and clear to handle at the surface. But when you try to avoid being true to yourself and deal with the surface first, it becomes complicated, and it will create even more complications.

You want to try your best to raise your children, but there is no such thing as that. Instead, you *be* you. That brings the simplicity and the honesty. This is what they will actually receive from you. They don't need your rules and regulations. They are a little bit of you, and they come from you, and they are like you. They need what you need.

In parenting, you are saying to deal with your own wants and needs first, not your children's wants and needs?

I am saying that your relationship with your children is what I call the surface. We all want a quick fix so our children can grow in a nice way and in a nice environment. But the thing that is lacking is our connection with our *own* self. We are trying to fix outside of ourselves. You need to bring awareness into yourself in every single way in order to be *you* first.

Okay, so what is it that we're not seeing in ourselves?

We are not seeing our own weaknesses, our own beliefs, our own wants. In any relationship we want honesty, and yet it doesn't really happen. You are not happy inside, but you are trying hard. You are trying your best to give your family happiness, but you are lying to yourself. You're not happy, and you're trying to be happy. You have to earn your own happiness first, and then you will not have to make any effort to make other people happy. Your household will be receiving what you are.

❧❦❧❦❧❦❧❧

My granddaughter comes to me to practice her piano. I want her to practice, and if I let her do what she wants (not practice), she just plays and talks constantly. But then I feel I am judging and correcting her.

It is because you are not paying enough attention to *your* wants. Spend more time being with *what* you want in this. This must come first, because this gives birth to everything else. You are seeing it, but now try to *be* with it until it dissolves, letting your wants happen. Letting it dissolve *in* you is most important. Don't try to touch the second part yet. You are thinking, "If I let go of expecting her to practice, then this is what will happen." That is your creation; that is not reality. You don't know what will happen yet. You have no idea, so you create your own belief in this. Allow yourself to go into the deepest part of that wanting in you, and that wanting will open up many more wants that you have. It will be a whole different story when you reach to your granddaughter again.

❧❦❧❦❧❦❧❧

My son is avoiding me, and I need him. I want to spend time with him. I know he loves me, but he won't talk to me, and I feel it is my fault.

You see that you are the one who is expecting something from your son. You are even saying aloud "I know he loves me," but you don't really trust that inside of you. Keep the awareness that you want to be direct with yourself at all times, and take a look at your expectations instead of looking at him. You are thinking, "How do I need to be with him?" or "How can I change him so he will be what I expect or want or need from him; how can I get his attitude toward me to change?" You don't need to change him, and you don't need to try to understand him. The more you try to understand him, the more you make him uncomfortable.

But when you are direct with yourself, not trying to understand him, you then will be in his feet and not his head. Be in his feet and in his shoes rather than his head. This will be a great help to you. You need to be grounded in *you* instead of giving power to your mind and power to your thinking all the time. The more you give power to your thinking, the more you make everything seem real for yourself, and then you keep rolling around in it, and that won't take you anywhere.

Well, he tells me he is drinking and partying to avoid his problems. I feel I am responsible to help him. I'm his mother.

I know, but you cannot help him in the way you are handling things. He is in his mental body and rolling around and around, and when you are also in your mental body, you are feeding him. Bring yourself down to where you don't need to understand him, and just trust, staying in his feet and not in his head.

In the last four months I haven't seen him very much.

Well, that's what I'm saying. You cannot fix the surface in others, but you *can* turn back inside of you. Children are not for us to hook ourselves into. Children can help us to grow deeper in and of ourselves. Everyone is in this same predicament. How can we fix others? Be thirsty for what is within *you*, not what is outside you.

❧❧❧❧❧

I see clearly how enormously contracted I am in every way when I am around my drug-addicted son, and I see that this is the very part of me that I can try to open up within.

92

Learn to enter the part (patterns) you're conscious of, and when you enter, the pattern will unfold. Always remember that in order to enter, you need to stay small so you don't threaten that part of you in any way. Also, become more and more grounded in the smallness; being grounded helps you to see more.

How does this noninterference play out with our children, whom we also have to guide?

On a certain level you can guide the child, but that guidance often depends on the parents' patterns and thoughts. Usually the parents want the child to follow their values and beliefs. This ends up in fear and control. When a parent begins to see his or her own fear, control, and patterns, that parent interferes less with the child's growth. Then the child has more freedom and can begin to think for himself or herself. The child can fall and learn, because he or she is going to fall anyway; that's life. Sometimes pushing your children will make them fall more. They need freedom to apply their own knowledge.

Sexuality

Could you talk with us about what sexuality means? It can cause so much pain, as well as joy. There are so many problems in our world associated with our sexuality.

Sexuality is a very strong component of human existence. People often try to push their sexual feelings away and try to put out their natural fire, which actually ends up fanning the flames. People need to be comfortable in their sexuality, and when they are more comfortable, slowly they will be able to go beyond sex and not be controlled by it or try to control it. The more one tries to stifle or put a lid on sex—or, on the other hand, participate in sex to excess—the more their sexuality will drive them.

Stay within the self and stay comfortable in your own sexuality. See it as it is. See it as just sexuality and that it is no bigger than you. Sexuality is big in this human existence because we are born from it. People lose control of their sexuality because they are feeding it, or they lose control because they are putting a lid on it. If people can be *still* within as they face their own sexuality, clarity will come. Sexuality is not bad; people just need to be more comfortable and stand straight within their sexuality.

Is infidelity a sin?

Society builds certain values and belief systems. The individual cannot really rebel against these values and beliefs without having judgments made about him or her by the outside world. People can decide within themselves how they want to express their sexuality. People make sexuality very big. Sex is naturally big, because that is how we are created, and that is also very big. When a natural part of existence is this big, people need to stay very small. Stay with your sexuality in a small way and a straight way. For example, if you see your jealousy in regard to a sexual matter, that is a good thing; see your jealousy and be with that.

As a counselor, I deal with people's intense feelings of betrayal, jealousy, and shame; so many intense feelings stem from the use or misuse of sex. Do we confuse love with sex?

People do not know about love. People think they know about love, but attraction is not love. Sexuality is not love. Love is such a high state, a pure state that a person can earn by being pure within. Love is a state of being; it is not applied or forced or manufactured. For example, parents say to children, "I really, really love you." But as these parents begin to see their huge investment in the child, the parents' wants, needs, ownership, interference, and fears abound. There are many things underneath what a person calls love. If all the fears, wants, and needs are removed, then the feeling about love is completely different. You don't feel love; you *are* love. If relationships can be cleaned from the ownership, fears, needs, and wants, then they can be beautiful.

So when we are melting more and more into love, does sexuality diminish?

Sex in a relationship is more beautiful when there isn't ownership, when there is no desire to change the other person and there is open acceptance of each other; then it's just a simple flow. Whether sex happens or doesn't happen is not a big deal; there is a flow between two people, that's all, and that flow becomes purer as each person becomes purer.

Is it wrong to have sex with a number of different partners?

It depends on what you know the truth to be. If it feels like dishonesty is within you, then you hold that dishonesty. It would better not to have sex if sex causes you to hold back in shame or dishonesty. That spoils your inner purity, and then you become a slave to it inside.

As a man, without my sex drive and without sex I feel less powerful or less empowered and not like a man.

One man said to me a while back, "You can't even imagine how big sex is to me; it's too big." Nothing needs to be so big. You don't need to carry, be driven by, or hold on to anything. Nothing is bigger than you; you can stand in anything. Standing firm in everything—that is your backbone. Hiding anything creates ugliness. Hiding one's sexual issues from oneself creates ugliness. Open up to look at it with your heart. If you feel guilty, open up that guilt and see what is there. If you feel enslaved, open up that slavery and see what is there (shame, guilt, desire, attachments, etc.), and keep doing that until you see.

Miscellaneous Questions

Many sacred scriptures talk about the importance of the physical human body. Isn't our awareness of heart more important?

If you do not have a body, you cannot do this learning and you cannot be awakened. When you shed your body, you are already, in a way, awakened. But the thing is, in that awakened state, you still carry your unrealness from physical lifetimes. The human body has all the qualities needed to fully awaken.

Does the mind have any place in spirituality? Can the mind be pure?

The mind isn't the problem in the first place; the person is the problem. When you want something, you train the mind; your greed or selfishness trains the mind. You have given power to the mind, and now you are learning how difficult it is to take power away from the mind. Instead, just see where you've given your power and let it be; just see your impurity in order to be pure.

Could you explain about dreams? What are they?

You don't have to depend on your dreams. As you change, your dreams change. They show you a little bit of realness, but they are temporary, shifting, and still unreal. Any picture you see in visions or dreams is not real. Dreams are a form of deeper thinking.

I want to ask a question about the chakras. Do they have any significance?

The chakras are another belief system. It's going to keep you going in circles. You believe you have to feel a certain way in your body, but that is temporary. Why do you want to start with something temporary? This learning is more direct. It's not about going into the chakras, into meditations, and into belief systems. It is about going directly into the heart that you know. Everybody knows about the heart. The heart is so simple and clear. But you don't want to trust your heart, and instead of trusting your heart, you start doing different spiritual practices. These practices are going to keep you busy, nothing more than that. Also, there is a danger in working with chakras because you can open up something that you may not be able to tolerate.

What are your thoughts about meditation?

There are many different ways to meditate, and each of them offers some parts that are good. Sitting with yourself is really nice, but it all depends on *how* you are sitting with yourself. If you are trying to avoid things outside of you and go into a comfort zone inside in order to avoid discomfort, that will not help you much. But if you have something bubbling up in you and you are willing to sit with it, the quietness will help you move through it to dissolve it. As long as you are not using any kind of meditation as a way to escape or to hold on too tight, then meditation is a good way to *be* with yourself. Use everything you can, even your meditation, to open yourself up and see within.

Do we experience multiple births, and if so, do we choose multiple births because it's familiar to us?

Yes, the person keeps experiencing many births. Some people don't want another birth, but it's not in their hands. You keep having birth after birth so you can awaken.

What if we've done inner work like we're doing here, but maybe we don't awaken. Would we carry over what we learn about awakening forward into future lives?

This is true inner growth. That is the only thing that stays with you in future births.

When my body leaves me, what happens to my heart? Does it go anywhere?

Formlessness stays with you.

Does it carry anything with it from a particular lifetime, and does the heart improve once it leaves the body?

It's not about past lives; it's about what you're carrying deep within you. The heart does not improve without a body.

Do you see many people awakening in the future? Will humanity start to awaken on this planet?

I can't visualize the future, but from the knowing, I do know that human beings are exhausted and that their deep fatigue is creating the pull to awaken within. I do see that people are tired of trying to change themselves. At this time, there is little exposure to this type of teaching to attain an awakened, self-realized state. Humanity has not—at least not on a large scale—been exposed to this type of teaching to awaken and to become self-realized.

All religions are basically the same in offering a path to salvation, but this teaching is different from religious learning. Could you talk about that?

Most religions began with an awakened, self-realized person. But from there, unawakened followers took it forward through time and created the dogma that exists today. The belief systems of these religions are not from the awakened teacher. Religious systems evolved from unawakened human beings who are asleep and living through their created self. Religions are driven by those people and those belief systems. Because of this, there is no awakened source point anymore, and no awakenings by the followers. Humans can't awaken from that; they need a crack—some way to enter their own created selves and see. This doesn't happen when beliefs and dogma come between the created self and the real self.

By coming to these meetings, one can see that these teachings are completely opposite from what most people have been taught for centuries. It feels threatening, and it *is* threatening to the person both knowingly and unknowingly. Some people don't continue with this teaching because their beliefs are stronger than their inner pull. Some people don't continue because their person doesn't want to be shattered and they are scared to be shattered. I always say that at the core of this learning, your pain is your true medicine and needs to be drunk by you even though it tastes bitter.

It is written in the Gurbani (scriptures), "Be in your pain." But this is not followed, because that belief system doesn't know what it really means. And yet even the devout keep running away from pain. A person is looking for a higher self or a higher power, but if your inner doors are protected, how can anything enter there? Protection means the heart gates are closed on every side. No crack—nothing can enter.

So, in this, first recognize that you are protecting yourself from everything. The only way to let down the walls, the guards, is to face directly what is within the walls.

This is *real*, this is big, this is not small, and this is not theoretical or metaphorical; it's literal. Whoever is willing can begin. I see that many who have that willingness and readiness are coming here. If a person can use that willingness to come to the meetings, then it begins to happen. I am showing people how to let go of their beliefs and showing them where they blindly believe. Beliefs are a cover. They do not help you to awaken; they just keep building more coverings, secretly.

How many have awakened from your teachings?

I don't want to go into that. In the past there were some who have easily awakened, and many of the other students made a huge deal about it, and this was not helpful to anyone. If you are in the sessions, then it is much more valuable to see that you, too, are on a level of awakening, because becoming awakened has many levels.

The Connections

The following pages are transcripts of connections that were recorded during various sessions with Gurpreet at retreats held across Canada in 2012 and 2013. During a connection, an individual sits in front of Gurpreet and asks questions on any subject that is important in his or her life.

What Is the Purpose of This Life?

I wonder what the purpose of my life is. I fulfill many roles and enjoy them, but there is still a void, and I feel disheartened. Can you tell me why I am here on this planet and what is the purpose for this life?

So there is one thing that you *do* know: living at the surface is *not* the purpose. With that knowing, you feel disheartened in your heart. That disheartened feeling is much deeper than what you have been living for. Being disheartened is your invitation to *be*. It is the door in front of you where you will be able to discover the real self.

You know that the things at the surface can be understood by your mind, but what is deep inside cannot be understood by the mind. You must be able to give all of yourself to those feelings of being disheartened in order to move toward the real self. Trust the truth of that little bit of knowing through your questioning, through that void. Trusting what you know of this little bit helps you *be* in more. You do know this, but you have been disconnected from that knowing for a long time. You need to reconnect with your knowing. Through that, you will recognize what is *not* real. The more you recognize that unrealness in you, the more it will help you to land in the realness within.

The knowing is helping you to recognize what is real. Even though you know only a little bit, that is enough to take the next step. It is not anything that is loud in you, but it is everything that is subtle in you. It is that. What is subtle in you is quite visible, and that is why you are not satisfied at the surface. Choose not to close your eyes to that subtlety in you.

Are We More than the Physical Body?

I've never been an emotional person and have experienced joy mostly through the physical things I've done. Is it okay for me to not be an emotionally based person?

It is absolutely okay if you are okay with it. There is nothing wrong with anything. But that is only if you *are* okay. If you are *not* okay, then maybe there is something you are blocking. See if you are blocking something painful or are in some kind of avoidance. If you have no avoidance, then it is fine; just let yourself expand in it knowingly, and let yourself *be* in it completely. Be curious, and don't let yourself be satisfied.

You are not curious enough about what is inside of you. This physical world is not what you are, and inside the physical body, there *is* somebody in there. That is what you need to be curious about—to see *you*, to meet that *you*. Meeting only this body is temporary.

I think my biggest fear is that a time will come when my body doesn't work anymore and it starts to disintegrate.

Yes, it's going to go; that is the reality. But are you facing that reality? You just mentioned there is fear and there is some kind of terror about the body dissolving. This is what you are familiar with, and what you are familiar with is what you become attached to.

Yes, big time.

So, instead of just seeing this physical attachment, see this fear. This fear will wake you up. Be with this fear; you don't need to push it down or pretend you don't have it. Bring that fear in front of you, and let it wake you up. Bring a little more reality into you and just be curious. Don't satisfy yourself, because satisfaction keeps you sleepy, and then you think only about this physical world. You think, "I am living with this physical body; this is what I am." This is *not* what you are, and even you know that. But this is so subtle. The person is so used to doing his or her work from morning to night and then saying, "Okay, I'm done for the day; tomorrow I will see another day."

Yes, that would be me.

You need to wake up to be a little bit more aware than that.

It sounds easy, but what does that entail? How do I wake up?

Recognize that you are saying, "I am happy about my life." But *are* you happy about it? *Are* you really, truly happy about it? You are just putting a lid there, and you are trying to make it happier. Look inside, because in truth you are not actually happy. Nobody is. You are not meeting *you*, so how can you be happy? Many people say to me, "I am a happy person." But these people cannot be happy, because they are not what they think they are.

You work from morning to night. You work and eat and go for a walk and have family time and this and that, but you *know* that there is still something missing—there is some sad point. Even though it seems very tiny, there is a sad point in you in this life that you lead. If you do find that sad point, then you will say, "Yes, nothing is satisfying me. I can work, I have my family, I have money, I have a house, I have everything, but still there is something missing." There *is* something missing; there is some kind of sadness showing in you.

So I should go into that?

Yes, go into that sadness. Your person keeps you busy so you don't go there. Your person thinks it's a bad thing and says, "I have to go on holidays to keep away from that sad point." You already know that this is not the key for happiness.

No, I've done that. I thought the secret for happiness was to go to Mexico in the winter and spend three months at a time on the beach. I had sun and no worries, but I got bored. It wasn't happiness; it was a created happiness.

Yes, created happiness is limited. Even if you build a house by the beach it will not serve the happiness. What you know about this is very, very true. Some people have a family and a whole lot of money—extreme money—and are rich in every way; they have everything, but still they are not happy. There is something missing. So what is missing then?

Is it heart?

It is *you* that is missing. This is the door to the higher self that you call heart or awareness. Knock on that door. Knock! Don't let yourself sleep in that worldly way.

That doesn't scare me in any way.

That is beautiful. That sadness is beautiful. If there is sadness and you are facing that sadness, so what? What is the big deal about it? Let yourself *be* in it completely. Open the door and let it in. Let whatever comes come. When you make a big deal about sadness or any negative feelings, a protective wall is built, and then the person lives only in the outside world. Discovering your true self is the most profound, endless way to happiness through that love and that joy. Everything is in it. This is endless; you cannot find any end.

That seems like a good start.

This is real. For example, the first thing that happens when a person leaves his or her body (in death) is that the person feels disappointed and wonders, "Why did I miss it? Why did I miss it again?"

Curiosity

This is my first time here. I don't really believe in much beyond mind and matter; I think I am here to suffer and enjoy, suffer and enjoy. I'm not here today to find answers, but I'm here to ask you what you see in me.

You want me to answer this for you? You said you came here out of curiosity. That's enough to start with. Through joy or suffering, you don't have your own ground. When you don't have your own ground, you're just being driven by joy and suffering. By finding your own ground, you become able to recognize that joy and suffering are not bigger than you. It's only when you're being driven by them that they become bigger than you.

Create curiosity to find your own ground where things don't push or pull you. That little curiosity helps you to be awakened, even from what is pushing and pulling you. Simply know you're being driven by the joy and suffering, in a sleepy way. Know that being in the sleep can be easy sometimes and it can be extremely difficult sometimes. That is why when difficulties come, you suffer and are torn apart. That tearing apart happens because of your sleepiness. You are much more than your joy or your suffering. That *more* is a big ocean in you; long to connect with it.

Isn't that painful in itself?

In the beginning it can be painful. The little pain in the beginning brings you to the permanent cure. It shows you how to swim in your own ocean, your own love. Otherwise, you will go in the pain again and again, which doesn't take you anywhere. Being disconnected from your own love is extremely painful; the person is not aware of this. Return and face that pain from your side. That lets you land in your own love and be softened in your joy and in your pain. That helps you to land back in you the soft way.

Where do I sign up? How do I start? How do I love myself without feeling pity for myself?

You sign up in your heart. Love yourself the soft way. Recognize and see your self-pity, and learn not to participate in it. Softly be in the kindness, because kindness helps you to reconnect in a direct way. Being kind and being soft are not your weaknesses; they are your strengths. Just trust that.

Talking

You have said that the less we talk the better, because it takes us away from our inner self. You said talking is a protection. How is that?

Talking unnecessarily shows you something you are not part of. When you talk more than you need to, there is dishonesty in that. You may find in the beginning that when you talk only when you need to, it creates a feeling that is uncomfortable in you because you are familiar with being the other way around. When you are talking when you feel like it, or when you are planning an event, socializing, and not being what you really are, see what opens up in you.

Speaking directly with only what you know is effective. The other big words—they are wonderfully shallow. If you continue to give energy to the shallowness, you will stay shallow instead of being real. Less is always better, in every way. In being less, there is nothing to lose. Bigness in words is like big balloons. You spend your whole life trying to move those balloons around carefully so they don't pop. But by being less, you don't mind any kind of needle around you, and the needle is wonderfully allowed, because in truth, there will be nothing that needs to be popped. Little by little, come to *like* being small by seeing the bigness, and be in the heart.

Little Star in Your Heart

I've always wondered if there was a true living master who could lead me out of this deep ditch. I now realize you are that teacher who can help me rid myself of my sorrows and medications and be awakened.

Yes, it is good to see you, and it is good that you are recognizing that you are in this rut. It's beautiful that you are exhausted and that you are seeing that you want to get out of the ditch. I love it when people recognize their exhaustion. It's a lovely recognition that will bring you to the teacher; otherwise, you wouldn't come. Keep trusting and keep loving. Let yourself be happy that you came here. It is like a tiny star in you. Let it shine. You came! Be happy for *you*. You came!

Keep that tiny star in your heart. You will sleep with that little star, and you will wake up with that little star. Slowly let it shine in you. All your sorrows, all your patterns don't matter. This little happiness and our meeting are meaningful to you. You will make it more meaningful when you stay connected with that star in your heart.

Without a true master, how can anyone be awakened? And to realize I have found you! I feel so very fortunate; my prayers have been answered.

Yes, isn't it lovely? It's like you have arrived somewhere. The star is beginning to shine in your heart, and it is so lovely. Now when you stay with that star all the time, you won't worry about your sorrows so much, and your energy will change by staying connected with that star in your heart.

Would you please look after me from now on?

Yes. You stay with that star in your heart. You said it; your prayers have been answered.

How Can I Self-Realize

I feel so much gratitude for your presence. How can I get to the place of self-realization?

Self-realization requires honesty.

How can I do that?

You do that by seeing how you have been stopping yourself. Do you have a tiny clue about what brought you here or how you are standing in your own way? Do you see how you have been dishonest with your longing? Have you been fair with yourself, or are you seeing your unfairness with yourself? Underneath that unfairness, there is a lot more for you to see. Be in that unfairness, and see and respect all the discomfort you face in it. Honestly be in it. You are being dishonest with yourself, and your dishonesty has created the unfairness. Instead of facing the unfairness, you are participating in it, and that creates even more unfairness. You want to go home or you want to be self-realized, but the cost is big, and you don't want to face it.

Can you show me how to face these things so I can go home?

Asking for it isn't enough. You have to decide from your heart and then stick to your decision. The more you ask for it and the more you don't do it, the more shallowness it creates in you. This keeps you occupied instead of just *being*. You are saying you think and believe inside of you that you will do it, but that isn't necessarily true. The more you believe what you are saying, the more you keep yourself in the darkness. As you recognize and see your unfairness with yourself, then from that point, see more dishonesty in every angle (part) of you. When you believe what you are saying, you then create your own fantasy. That fantasy is always wobbly. Being in the unfairness shows you much more that is not real. Be ready to see it—not just in a shallow way, but in an honest, desperate way. Anything you can use, use it as a wake-up call.

111

What you are asking for, give core value to it; otherwise, you will continue to satisfy yourself by saying and believing what you are asking for. You don't need to cover your feelings and emotions, and there is no need to create self-importance in you. This is how you create the unfairness within you. Nothing is in your way except for you. You need to see that as you become more honest; then you will face your own pain. It is worth being in the pain, and it is much better than covering it up. When you see your own pain, do not run away from it; instead, honestly embrace the pain. There is a door to enter with the same honesty; don't let any pain leave. Every dishonesty, every pain within, is worth being in. Love to lay down your powers and be in the powerlessness and be more direct with your unfairness.

Can you explain that, please?

Using your own power, mental power, is a protection. The more you protect yourself, the more you stay blind to your real self. The more you are powerless, the closer you are to your unfairness and the easier it is to see. Anything that is creating a distance in you, see that. The more you are willing to see with deep, core honesty, the more you will be able to see. As you are able to see, stay honest. But you need not change; just embrace without judgment.

The Heart

I am confused about what you mean by the heart.

It is the person that is confused about what heart means. Just remember that the heart is a center, and knowing that, come closer to the center rather than being confused and scattered. When you are scattered, then the level of being in the heart changes, but you *do* know the *true* way of being in the heart. As you are in the heart, include everything that touches your heart. You feel confused because in a split second you can be out of the heart again.

By returning again and again to being in the heart, you will slowly increase your awareness. As your awareness increases, include little by little everything you see. You have a lot of capacity to include everything. The person can carry huge piles of scattered energy—unnecessary and unimportant things—and this can make you feel that you do not have the capacity to be in the awareness. These unimportant things are a lot to include, especially when you are unaware that you are scattered. But as you remove that scatteredness, you see more and more of your dishonesty, which brings you lots of disappointment and discomfort; it's worth being in it, rather than the other way around.

So what about laughter?

See what is underneath the laughter. Are you covering something up? If you look, you will always find what you don't want to see.

As I am saying this, what is it like to you?

I think I'm feeling sad that I have not been in awareness.

That is way better. Your heart is happy that you recognize that you're feeling sad. Sadness is more precious than your laughter because it is underneath. That is a glimpse of how the person covers all of life. It does not want to give you the truth. When you are disappointed or sad inside, the old way of being will tempt you to laugh. You now know it's not real. Step-by-step, you will come to see the unreal part of the laughing. Don't touch its grief, and don't act as if nothing is wrong; just *be* with it. It is touching your heart because it's your heart longing that you have neglected. Now it's coming up, and a little of the realness is shining through. It actually is shining a lot more than the amount of the unrealness. This is how you discover yourself. Step-by-step, increase your awareness every moment.

Recognize that reality is not selectiveness but broadness. When you are selective, you go into likes and dislikes. In this there are no dislikes. Everything is welcome regardless of how it looks or how you feel.

Recognize that there is sadness, and see that it doesn't feel good. As you recognize it, be okay to be in it. The feeling does not matter. When you go with the feelings, you become selective, and as soon as you become selective, you are not going to let the realness come to the fore. Being real does not feel good at all, but being real is permanent. As you become aware of feelings, just include them in your heart. As you do so, regardless of how you feel, they will really, really open your heart. Then the real laughter comes, and that laughter will touch your heart in realness.

Staying with the Heart
in Daily Life

When I am doing my job, I am in my mind, and in order to come back into my heart, I have to stop what I'm working at. When I try to stay in my heart, I stop being in the outside. How can I do both?

Instead of trying hard, just give yourself little lovely reminders throughout your day to be in the heart. Trying doesn't let you be in the heart, and when you are trying to be in the heart, the trying itself paralyzes you. Being in the heart takes simple awareness, and that awareness also tells you when you're not in the heart. As you remind yourself to come back to your heart, you will become more and more aware of how to treat yourself. You will become lighter with yourself instead of living in a heavy way. When living with heaviness, everything seems heavy. Instead, naturally go into everything, and when you are being with everything, know where you are. When you are working at your job, just simply come back into you.

Yes, but that's the problem. If I'm not in my mind, I can't perform in the work world.

Learn to be in the *new* way, which you know is true for you to be, and value being in your heart. Value being in your heart rather than thinking, "I can't do it." Simply do whatever you need to do on the surface. Being in your heart is a natural way of being; this is not something unusual. What *is* unusual is believing you cannot do anything else besides be heart-full. Love *being* in the heart, but know that it does not mean *having* to be in the heart. Being in the heart in this lovely way doesn't carry any weight. Instead of trying to come back, stay with what you love in your heart; love the space you're in. Love this natural way and the want will drop. Instead of giving up, just remind yourself many times every day to do this. You may not get the same space that you have here, but you will be with yourself with the same love. Trust your *own* love that you have in this space. You will be awakened in your *own* love. Love what you have in you.

I feel like I am a failure when it comes to being in the heart.

Now you are at the core of the problem. Being a failure feels too loud, and you are letting that be as loud as it wants, so you end up losing your love. It's natural that every weakness of yours is going to be louder than before because you're touching it—touching it with the love. The weakness doesn't want to diminish in you, but remember, you don't want to kill it. Just gently allow that weakness to come in you. Be fully aware that you are opening the door to your weakness as you are letting love be. It's just wonderfully okay. It is just the taste that is not great.

As the weakness enters, it is normal that you may tremble with it. It's okay; love that it is entering. Let it open up in you completely. Actually, look for more corners to see where that weakness may be hiding. (Be aware of every little thought and feeling all the time.) You can see weakness easily. This is how you are able to become naked in your weakness. As you become naked, you'll see weakness everywhere. That is the beginning of the end of this weakness. Don't criticize yourself in any way; just choose to enter everywhere. When you choose to be everywhere inside you, that will change your interior. You are opening up much more than before, and as you open up, your old habits will tell you to go to sleep again. Be responsible to this opening, and do not fall asleep. Even when you've closed your door on a weakness, remember to open that door again and to do so with joy and love.

Inner Peace

How does one get inner peace?

Real peace is earned by paying the cost. For example, real peace does not get disturbed by others, and you have to lose the attachment to what you want from others. Those attachments are part of a pattern in you, so enjoy seeing your patterns. Quieting the thoughts is not real peace, because thoughts are shallow, and even though you may manage to quiet them, you do so only on the surface. You need to go deeper into your heart. It is not necessarily when you close your eyes that you deepen; even when you are working, talking, or walking, you can deepen. Stay in your heart.

To gain real peace, you have to first move through all your unpeaceful parts, and that does not feel good. But if you have an honest thirst about this, then you won't mind doing it. If you have a strong thirst, it will continue to pull you toward realness. To be in the real self, you have to move through your unreal self.

When somebody pokes you and you become disturbed, that is good, not bad. It can appear bad, but this is showing you what is within you and what you are seeing inside yourself. *Like* being with that and embrace it. This is the process one has to go through. A person has to move through all the patterns and all the impurities he or she has created within. You have to move through all of them with your eyes open and wonderfully accept it all.

Pure heart is the real peace. Pure heart does not know its purity; it only sees its impurity. In anything, when you think you have earned either purity or peace, you actually haven't yet. You can use this to measure yourself to move forward, because the person measures the opposite way. When you see you are *not* pure or peaceful, then you actually *do* have it a little bit, because that little bit of purity in you is seeing it.

Real peace is not recognized with mind understanding; walking in the heart is very different. The mind likes to build (even peace or purity), and the heart does not. The heart does not build anything. It does not filter anything. The heart only knows to move as is. The heart does not mind the cost; the filtering comes when the person does not want to pay the cost and wants to save itself. When you stand straight, your heart does not mind. The heart knows and accepts everything, no matter what anything looks like. Right now your heart is burning, so give lots of room to it and just allow whatever happens. It is when you don't allow that conditioning takes over and the unrealness goes on and on. *Like* yourself no matter what you see or what you are in. Be kind to yourself regardless.

*Looking for Peace
or Looking for Truth?*

I am feeling very peaceful right now, and I don't want to lose it.

Are you looking for peace, or are you looking for truth?

What is the difference between peace and truth?

An experience of peace is not permanent; you don't want to lose it, but whatever you hold on to is smaller than you.

I want to go beyond that.

Then don't touch any kind of feelings of peace.

What do you mean by that?

You are saying, "I don't want to lose it," which is what you are experiencing now. But you are already putting your hand in it. If you experience peace, it is not a bad thing; like it, and be in it as is. But that is not for you to hold on to. The real peace comes when you are not experiencing peace. This takes place solely in the heart. In the heart there is no want and no need for peace. You just be as is, detached but longing to continue to integrate that detachment.

After this morning's session, I went home and went to sleep. Even in my sleep I was experiencing changes within my system.

You are changing, and you earned it. You tasted it, and because of the taste much is happening in your system; it is real. But after this taste is gone, the want comes: "I want this, and I don't want that." Even though there is so much happening in your system, it still needs the cleaning process. You may be able to experience this longer, but earning it is still required.

But in this peace, I don't want to do anything. Again, that wanting—is it wrong?

First value this. When you are experiencing peace, be in it without touching it. (Enjoy the peace without hanging on to it or wanting to stay.) Not touching it will bring more awareness in you. Touching it and making it yours will make you blind in the pattern. As soon as you go into the pattern, you lose the truth of it. Your openness is beautiful, and in this openness a lot more steps need to be taken in order to earn more. While you are in it, fully enjoy it; fully be in it. Because you have your head down, all the way down, this experience is just your invitation for the walk. But never expect any kind of experience, even in this, to happen again.

I am feeling very peaceful right now.

Keep one aim. Instead of choosing peace *and* truth, choose one.

I choose truth.

Then let go of the peace. Truth costs everything. The cost is greater, and you pay the greater price, but the earning is also greater.

I'm feeling something here.

The little bit you do know, you cannot put into words because it is still so small. Truth is totally formless; you can't experience it. Anything that has boundaries, you are able to experience. But then it is not real; it is only temporary. In this, you'll feel like you are going backward, because it is totally opposite according to what you know. Embrace that shattering and be free from your own ideas about truth.

Anytime you feel like you've got it, that means you haven't. Be in that knowing, and then you're able to be free from your own ideas. Truth is not your business. The untrue part of you is your business, and you should wonderfully be in it. When you are in it, just watch as your hands come out to touch instead of fooling yourself that you are not touching. When you say, "I'm not touching," you are limiting yourself.

Be broader in the seeing. When you are being in it honestly, you'll really be surprised. The honest seeing (truth) doesn't care about the cost and the feelings, but person (ego) does. Being in the seeing of dishonesty is not bad at all. That actually will help you in every way.

Being in This World

I have been spiritual for many years, but I feel I am being very hard on myself because I have one foot walking this path and one foot in the world. What can I do to make this easier?

Instead of easier, choose possible. There is no such thing as easy. When you decide to make it possible, then you face the difficulties, and if you stay firm in that decision, you will be able to move through the difficulties. The easy way is *your* way, and you don't need that.

So how do I be in the world but not of the world?

When you try to remove yourself from the world, you cannot do it, because there is pain and disappointment, and you don't like that. Anything you don't like, you will secretly carry within you. Start from wherever you are in the world, and see what the world is showing you inside of you. The root of the world is in you. The world is not the cause. The root is in you; in creating.

Being in the root is difficult, even when you know what the cause is, and *being* in the cause is difficult. It's not that visible for you because you are busy participating in it, and that's okay, but choose to stay within by being kind to yourself. With the kindness, you are able to take in the world you don't like. As you are able to take it in, you become able to embrace what was causing difficulty on the surface. By embracing, you become able to go to the root little by little. Going to the root is like letting your will be lifted. When your will is lifted, you feel uncomfortable because you're not used to such nakedness. But continue to learn to be okay in such nakedness. Being in the little bit of nakedness is the start toward the inner world you have created, and that way you learn to live to purify yourself instead of living for spirituality.

Let yourself sink and sink forever. This sinking will give you birth one day, and then you will let the newness be born. That newness knows how to live in the same world you've been running from. The sinking is able to remove what you've been carrying within you. Sink without reason. In the sinking, you lose, but it's not real. Trust what you are instead of believing what you think you are. What you are, you don't understand. What you believe you are, you are trying to fix. Just let your ship sink. There is no way out. Dearly face the reality, and live in this dearness. This dearness always helps you. This is your possibility. Now you know, because you see. This plugging in is forever.

So how do I stay plugged in?

By giving your whole self to your possibilities, little by little. This might bring many doubts, but you cannot deny what you're seeing and knowing. This plugging in is the invitation. By giving yourself to this, you learn little by little. In this plugging in, keep coming, regardless of what you lose. Regardless of the difficulties and regardless of how you're being torn apart, just keep coming.

So keep coming here and staying plugged in?

When you plug into the formlessness, you have no choice but to drop everything (all attachments, wants, needs, patterns, and beliefs.) Then you don't focus on plugging in; you just love losing everything for it. Dropping everything means you are walking toward the formlessness, which you know you're seeing even though you cannot understand it. Your habit is to try your best to understand what you're seeing. Dropping everything enables you to enter. That entrance is just a beginning, and then you endlessly walk.

Spiritual Practices

I have done many spiritual practices, such as chakra work, lots of meditation, yoga, breath work, and chanting. Which one is the most effective?

None of them.

Then how should one practice to progress?

Purity of the heart is first. Then any practice you like to do will be relevant. Until you have purity of heart, nothing you do will work. It might feel as though it is working, but it is not.

How do you become pure of heart?

First of all, have honest willingness and like to be pure at any cost. Being pure does cost; it costs everything inside of you and outside of you. In being pure, you don't get anything; you lose everything. No mental practice will make *real* movement in the heart.

Your willingness will show you your issues, your wants, and your needs, and as you bring kindness to those things, you can open up. In being pure, you lose all your investments. The techniques you mentioned are easy because you don't lose anything. In fact, when using these techniques, you are in the want of gaining something. These techniques can be done all your life, but you will still stay thirsty. When you are in these techniques, you create another pattern of *doing* instead of *being* in the heart.

You don't need to do anything at all. You see, doing is harder than not doing. Doing something to achieve—anybody can do that. Purity of the heart is everything. It needs nothing and wants nothing; it just merges as is. These spiritual techniques can easily help you to escape from yourself, but you cannot escape from yourself with this teaching, and this can wonderfully open you up.

I have no advice for you. It's just your choice to choose the "bold way." Within you there is something your person recognizes, and it is threatening. Even though this touch you have had within is small, it is very effective. Instead of taking any kind of advice, recognize the tiny bits that have been touched within in you.

Recognizing the Created Self and the Real Self

Every feature, every characteristic of my personality is all part of my created self, and it's mutated into something rigid and inauthentic. How can I distinguish between what is my created self and what is my real self?

Within you there is a tiny bit of recognition that in the life you are living, there is something missing. There is something that you label as you, but there is no truth in it. That much you do know; and what you do know within, let it land in you. That really will stir up everything in you, because that little bit of recognition knows that this is *not* reality. This will bring forth real sadness in you. That sadness is deep in you. When you let yourself be in the sadness, that itself will help you to see how many different ways you are still hanging on to the old self.

I feel very familiar with that sadness. Is that the created self?

Yes. What you are experiencing within lets you face this unrealness in you. In facing this unrealness, there is no right or wrong; just let it land in you instead of hanging in that. Hanging in it creates stress in you and doesn't let you be in the sadness fully.

I find it hard to think that freedom lies in submission.

Just start doing this in little ways, not too much at once. Too much will confuse you and won't let you be in anything. Start with a little bit of sadness, and learn to be in it fully. That can bring you so much truth. You don't need freedom first. Learn to be in everything that you have created in you, little by little. Be in the little bit you trust instead of trying to be in all of it at once.

In letting this land in me, will I recognize it? Can I distinguish it from the mind's logical thinking?

In letting yourself *be,* you'll see how many different ways interference will come from the created self. It's very hard to *be* in sadness for a long time. Just know that there *is* sadness in you. Being fully in it is something you learn. In this letting, you learn to trust in the little bit in you, but not with mind understanding because you can't use mind understanding for this walk. You just need to trust, and from the trust, you will know. That little trust is big. That will help you to go back again and again into the knowing. In that trust, there is no mind involvement. You are just *being,* regardless of what you lose in you.

Does it make you better adapted or worse?

It will seem like it is worse, but it's not bad. That sadness is your invitation to be true with yourself. That sadness is your invitation; it is your calling. Because of what you will be losing, you won't feel good. When you give no preference to your feelings and learn to give preference to your calling, it becomes easier.

Recognizing Falseness

I am caught in duality sometimes. I have to make a choice, but I don't know which option to choose. I often prefer both, and then I worry that I am going to make a wrong choice.

Right or wrong, neither option is you. In any preference or avoidance, neither option is you. When you are trying to choose either one of them, you gain no results. By seeing this, go deeper in you. You are only able to go deeper when you know that everything you are participating in at the surface is not you. There is no gain even if it is the right choice. It's not you. Recognizing all falseness is helping you to be in the deep.

Then just stop playing on the surface?

Yes, but only when you stay with the longing to go deeper. When you connect, and when you know what is true for you to be, it won't let you play with the falseness. As you recognize the falseness, don't be hard on yourself; instead let yourself be softened in it in every way so that you can be deeper. The falseness will continue to appear in many forms, but choose to go deeper regardless of what it is costing you. Being in the deep, you do lose your familiarities. As you lose all these false beliefs and your many investments, choose to be little. Then, slowly, you learn to give no preference to anything, and at the same time you welcome everything. (You have no judgments, likes, or dislikes.) By welcoming everything, it will help you to diminish in everything.

This is a great place to start. There's a lot there.

It is a lovely start when there is a yes from the deep. Even though you don't understand what that means in the mind, inside of you there is that yes from the deep.

Seeing the Person to Awaken

I feel I am at the border to awakening. How can I cross over? My work is limiting me, and I take days off because I don't want to be there anymore and I need more vitality.

You need to earn it. Your ground is ready. In order to earn it, you have to go through your whole created self. You can taste the vitality, be in it for a while, but it is not permanent because you have not gone through what you have created. You have to see everything and let go of everything. You have not seen your mechanics yet. Taking a day off for no reason is showing you how mechanical your behavior is. Knowingly be aware and see everything you are by going inside and seeing your habits, patterns, and belief systems. This is how you pay the cost that is required. Cost is everything.

Your work is not in the way; it is the way you are holding on to the work that is in the way. As you see that and be in that, you will open up to everything you do. It will show you the same pattern. Recognize where the true value is, and as you recognize the value, be in that value and stand in that value. Pay the cost.

I feel I am at the border of reality, and I want to cross, but I am still here.

Wanting to cross is longing. There is no doubt about that. The part that can't cross the border is your person. Be interested in the person, which cannot cross, rather than thinking about and longing for crossing the border. You can't ignore the person to get to the other side. See the person. Even though you keep trying to see the person, you keep failing. It seems very close because your ground is ready. To cross, you need the whole of you; you cannot leave the person behind. It is heavy.

I tried to leave the person for a fraction of a second. I saw that a little bit merged, but I am not sure.

This means you are just starting. You can't see the whole person right away; it is a process. If it were easy, the space you are longing for would have no value. You felt the closeness because you're grounded in the longing, but you see that a lot of embracing needs to be done. You are turning your face toward reality, and facing the reality of the created self is not easy. Facing this reality will shatter everything—all your thinking and believing up until now. It is heartbreaking as you allow this to happen. This walk is a walk toward the reality. It will change your whole interior. Begin with today.

How to See More

How can I see more of my created self?

Quietly be kind to what you see when you are in it. Do not give any room to "poor me" or attach any kind of self-importance. As you are quietly being in it, be even broader in your seeing. Take in more with your inner eyes. In being broader with your seeing, you will gain even more permission to see and more willingness to see. Then you won't be shocked. Each issue within you will become more and more open. Even go in the corner of the issue and look for more patterns and emotions attached to your issue by being and seeing.

Attaining More Awareness of Patterns

How can I earn more awareness about my patterns? I feel complacent.

Being in any pattern with awareness will really open you up. Patterns are very tricky. You can't see the pattern clearly, but you know you have a pattern. You are suffering, and so you shut down right away. Even when you pray to see a pattern, you are only just praying. You see a pattern in your memory and say, "Yes, it is there," but then you shut down again and lose sight of it. Be happy to keep the window open, and have lots of willingness to see. The pattern will open up in you again, and you can be fully in it again. Be not so much wanting to see it, but be willing to see it.

Do this step-by-step, and when your willingness increases, you will be fully in the pattern and fully honest being in it. To do this, there must be no wants and no needs—not even wanting to get rid of the pattern. Once you are in the pattern, it seems as though it is the first time and your eyes are opening up everywhere. Look and see how that pattern is there but your awareness is not. Being in the pattern will really show you how you have been managing that pattern in your life. You can do this if you have desperation and fire-full longing to see it. The real fire-full longing makes you feel as though you are sitting on a bed of fire and you have no way out so you are just surrendering to the fire. That much is needed.

How can I bring more desperation and fire-full longing?

By not getting satisfied. If you satisfy yourself by thinking you have enough desperation, then it's not enough. Desperation is there all day and all night, regardless of who you're with or what you are doing. If you are with that fire-full desperation all day long, you'll take it into the night too. If you see you are "kind of" with the fire-full longing, you'll

132

keep yourself blind. When you are really desperate for the "true way," there is no separation between you and desperation. Then you really know you are really thirsty, and the cost of the person isn't an issue anymore. When you give yourself permission to take a step *in*, that lets your person know, and that grants you permission for the next step. Give your whole self to it.

Being in Your Patterns

Today it is difficult to turn off my mind.

Even if you do, it will be temporary.

How can I be more in my heart?

With honesty, turn back. Turn back to where you do *not* like to be. Because that makes you uncomfortable, you keep trying to be in the comfort. Do not fight with anything. When you fight, you may temporarily think that you have relief from it, but it's just in your thoughts. In reality you won't change anything.

I want to be in that natural state of being awake. Why is it so easy here with you and so hard when I am by myself?

When you are by yourself you are trying to be in a better place rather than in what is there already, and you fight with that. Your wanting does not change anything. You say, "I want to be natural," but you do not know what is underneath the issue. When the issue is there, you cannot be natural. Right now you are tasting what it is like to be natural, and in order to be in this taste, you have to like to go where you don't want to go inside of you.

You must like going into your patterns and your wants and needs. You cannot skip all these parts of you and become natural. Being natural is earned. Being natural is what you originally were. But the things you have accumulated are in your way now. You cannot skip the smallest issue (pattern, want, or need) within you in order to be natural.

So how do I get out of those patterns and get them out of my way?

With real honesty. Give yourself gentle permission to be in the pattern. It doesn't matter that there are many patterns or if you want to run away *because* there are so many patterns. There are many wants and needs to look at. Shutting that door and running away from them in pursuit of the natural way is, in reality, a way of accumulating more issues. That's why it's important to turn back. Give gentle, honest permission to be okay in the pattern. Bring each pattern in front of you so you can be in it. When you gently allow yourself to be in the pattern, it will gently start opening up because it's not scared of you anymore. Then you are able to see you were just outside of that pattern.

Be gentle and soft toward that pattern, and don't fear it. Go into the middle of it (by seeing it and being it with awareness), where there is nothing else but you and your pattern. Stay in it continuously, and be as comfortable as you can be. The pattern will open up your inner eye, which you couldn't see before. One pattern can take you really, really deep within you and will show you that it is just you; it isn't about anything else at all, regardless of how you feel about it.

Just embrace any pain you feel from the pattern. It only hurts if you make a big deal about it, and if you don't make a big deal about that pain, your inner gentleness will grow more and more, and that will become habit. When you don't like the pain, then that will cause you to tighten again. As you introduce the gentleness, it removes the tightness. Every moment, introduce the gentleness, even if it has lost its way of surfacing. The pattern will try to distract you because now you are doing the opposite of what you used to do. Just stay in that little bit that you are moving into.

I have a burning in my heart.

You can allow even more burning in the heart. Even the pain in the heart will give more room for it. Pain is welcome as you introduce the gentleness. Continue to welcome the pain, and continue to lay your head in okayness in pain. Love being in that process; it's not killing you, and it's actually making you more alive.

Your issues help you. They are only your enemy when you have turned your back on them. When you turn your face toward your issues in a friendly way, everything helps you. Keep your willingness alive to go into every issue. You have heart intelligence within you that gives you the ability to do that. Just give yourself to it and walk with more fire within than before. How do you feel now?

It's not so painful after all.

And now be a friend with the pain. When you are a friend with the pain, then you are able to go into the heart of the pain.

It feels like there is no pain.

Bring more desperation to go into the patterns so you can open up every issue.

Why do I feel like I cannot do it on my own?

You did it so quickly here. You have the capacity, and you have the intelligence—heart intelligence. Trust that you can do it on your own, because you did do it here. It's like you met your lover and the lover touched your whole heart. So be in that when you leave here, because you do know that this is what you are in love with. When you are home, you will not forget the touch of it. Even when you go to bed it's not leaving you, because the touch is deep within you.

It's not something you can't do, because there is nothing *to* do but just give your kind permission. Giving your kind permission will give you the willingness to move through whatever comes. Move through the discomfort when it comes. You *are* moving through things that you have never liked before. This is freeing you. Once you free yourself from even one little pattern, as you did just now, the pull increases within you. You see that the pull has increased already. Be honest and comfortable when you see you are uncomfortable. Your discomfort removes the layers that you are covering up. How dear this is. Does the cost matter?

Nothing matters.

Then give your heart to it.

It feels amazing. It's so easy.

It *is* worth giving your heart to this. Just be in the seeing. When you are in the seeing, you may earn sweetness, and if amazement comes, know it's not for you to grab. It can be there or it can fully go away. Just enjoy seeing more and more. Love giving permission more and more, and like being in the seeing as the discomfort comes. Be okay in it.

As you learn to give your heart to this, the quality of your tears will change, and as those tears start touching you, you will be able to taste the love. As I'm speaking right now, you are walking, and if you continue to love walking, it will change you.

As you give your heart to this, your personal and impersonal will become one. Giving the heart is unlimited; the more you give, the more it feels like it's not enough. As you become able to give your heart and learn to live from the heart, then that will become a new way of being. And trust without analyzing anything. If you trust the heart, you will taste the goodness of the heart; your fear of losing is the only thing keeping you from this goodness. The more you don't mind losing, the more you will be deeply rooted in the heart.

The heart is everything. The heart is God. The heart is existence. Love being pure in it, and you will be all of that. You are only able to discover this when you trust without the fear of losing. The heart has endless vastness and endless depth. Love integrating all this.

So now what is the day going to be like?

Pretty incredible, I think.

I guess the night will too. As you make this as "living water," you will continually increase.

Falling into Old Patterns

I keep falling back into my old patterns. At least now I am beginning to see a lot more often that I am in a pattern. I need your help to discern more and untangle more.

Keep being in your heart, and stay with the heart honesty, where you don't need to get rid of anything. Love to see everything in you in an honest way. When there is heart honesty, the more you be *as is,* the less you will disturb or threaten your person. It's easy to see through what is bothering you at the surface, and this easily lets you enter within. By wonderfully being in it, you allow everything to open up in you without questioning it. When you're not busy questioning, then you can be more in it and let it happen more powerlessly. You are not controlling; instead, you are allowing. The feeling is not going to be good in that allowing. In that allowing, you lose your control. Allowing yourself to lose brings discomfort. Discomfort makes the person want to close the door and pretend it's not happening. That's where you need a great deal of awareness to recognize the discomfort.

I see the person dissolving. I don't see discomfort, but I do see a fear of dissolving because the person knows it's dissolving. There is some joy and some fear. I see both clearly.

Then pay the cost (letting go of attachments) and move forward. Let your heart open, and just recognize that you are okay. Do this comfortably. When you are ready to pay the cost, every single thing is possible in this.

Your presence is helping me. I want this to be a permanent change, so what should I do?

There are many layers to the person. Every time you see the fear of losing, stay with it in a friendly way and be okay to lose. By being okay to lose, you can stay in the fear of losing in a delightful way. When you come out of the fear, recognize what is causing you to come out so you can learn more about yourself in a kind way. Even when you're ready to pay the cost, the tricks are still there. Choose to stay in the deep; you'll earn more clarity. The softness and the kindness will relieve your knots. The more you release, the more you will be able to dissolve into your heart. Diminishing in the deep is the only way of being. Don't keep any other choice alive, and lose every bit of your old way of living, but do not do so in order to gain something. Lose only because it's so true to be. Then you will diminish in a true way.

You've made it so easy. Your presence is so intense, and I know that I just have to get into the practice of it. Why do I cry so much when I'm here?

Isn't it okay to have some tears of love? You know where you are going and love where you are going; just trust. You are always welcome. Melt in this love as much as you like, as every tear is washing you with grace.

Is it faith that is required to be able to take this leap?

It's a calling. It's your invitation to be what is real in you.

Is there something I have to be?

No. You are already experiencing your sadness; this is a starting point for you. This is a stepping-stone to the unknown in you, which you will move toward as you learn to trust. Because you are already experiencing sadness, it's easy for you to be in that sadness, and through that you can begin to enter.

How do I know this won't become another aspect of the created self?

Learn bit by bit. It's not something that drastically takes you to the other side. Walk in it from your side. In the walk, with every step, you will know that you are going forward into the unknown. You will know even though you won't understand where you are going. Just move forward in trust. Trust will take you beyond your created self.

The real self is not familiar to you in the beginning, but as you begin to trust, you will earn clear knowing in you and you will really move forward. Start because of your calling. There is no mind understanding

139

at this point, and this can feel completely opposite from "right." Just keep walking; you know there is no truth in what you have already created. What you have created is not nurturing you anymore. In you, the calling is not small; it's big inside of you. Because it's big, it doesn't matter how much you try to run away. And if you *do* try to run away, it will really tear you apart, because you know. When it's beyond your person, you can only trust through your heart, through the inner knowing. What touched you yesterday is already multiplying today.

I feel the pull toward this walk is strong in me.

Yes, because you're not too far away from it, and you taste it, and what you are tasting is not hard for you to trust. Give everything you have to what you taste. Throw yourself in this water. Then you will slowly realize it's not possible to live without this water.

Embracing Patterns

I want to talk to you about standing straight in what I know to be true.

Believing what you know to be truth, little by little, will ground you. But don't try to be grounded; don't try to go deeper. Believing and standing straight in it will remove the uncertainty. Be more aware within yourself, and whenever you're not in your heart, don't worry about it; with no judgment, come back into the heart again. The mind does not need to understand this.

I know what a lot of my patterns are, but I sometimes go into denial, and then I am upset with myself.

You see yourself doing that, and so you give yourself a hard time, and that begins a chain reaction. Soften yourself in the heart at the same time you are being in the heart. Gently see how your hands are busy doing that which you no longer need to do. You don't need anything, and in order not to need anything, you have to see that you are in your needs and wants. Gently be in them without any understanding. When you don't need anything, you don't need to do anything. But this brings up discomfort and doubts. That is why you are tempted to go back to *doing,* and again you begin to give yourself a hard time.

I don't understand that.

There is nothing to do. Bring all of it in front of you now, and allow everything as it is; as you allow this, everything will come up. Give lots and lots of room to it.

Yes. Embrace it.

Very tenderly and gently continue. By doing this, you will open; the tender embracing will open you up. When you open up, tenderly embrace. Continue to embrace with awareness without touching anything, without wanting anything. Tenderly embrace, and then ride joyfully. Your hands can wonderfully rest, fixing nothing. Seeing that pattern is very good, even if you only see the corner of it.

I love that.

When you see the corner of your pattern, embrace it and open up to it even more. Don't scare your pattern, because right now you are only embracing the corner. Even if you lose the corner, be in the willingness to see it again. Bring that pattern back, knowing that you don't need to fix anything. You are just tenderly embracing the pattern. Let the building fall; it is falling now. That beingness is much more real and is so natural when the building of familiarity is gone. Regardless of the feelings of discomfort or feelings of emptiness, just stay in the embracing.

No more playing hide-and-seek. What is it like now?

I am very open and really empty; it is like my feet are dangling in my heart. My knowing is very clear.

Even in this broader view, just stay in the tender embracing.

Nothing to Change,
Nothing to Fix

I wasn't clear on how to see myself, but I have more clarity now.

This is the first time that you have seen this lovely clarity.

I was missing seeing the patterns, and I was always looking for what was coming next. I'm going to stop doing that.

No. Now you are fixing again. This clarity that is opening up in you is a lot. It is only the mind that is telling you what is coming next. What has opened up in you is in your care. So first *be* in it, and you will see a lot more. If you convince yourself that what you were doing has to stop and you have to stop missing your patterns, then you will be doing the same thing again in a different way. Don't look at the next thing; only look at what has opened up in you *now*, because in that opening there is nothing to do. The old way wants to *do* something in that clarity. The *true way* is to enjoy your clarity and be in it.

I see that, but the mind comes on so strongly.

The mind comes on strongly because you are used to fixing things. Now there is nothing to fix, so it is hard for your mind to stay in that pause, because that pause has never happened before. This is very new for your system to handle, and so discomfort comes when you don't do anything to fix it. You now have clarity, and living in that clarity will be more difficult. That clarity you have is new, and your whole system will try to convince you in all sorts of different ways to move away from it. In that clarity, you feel like a failure, in a way, because the clarity is not being dealt with according to what you believe. Going down into the deep means swallowing the bitterness, and that's when the trickiness comes in. The only thing you can do is allow the discomfort.

As an example of this discomfort, imagine that you are in your house and you are sitting at the kitchen table. Someone starts to cook dinner, and you see that this person is very clumsy, and whatever he or she is making, you know you could make it better. But you have been ordered to sit; you are not allowed to move, and you have to watch the whole process. You cannot leave, and you can't ignore a thing. You are seeing everything being done wrong in accordance with the way you think it should be done.

You can imagine what would be going on inside you during this ordeal. This is how it works within your mind. The mind will come in again and again. It does not offer a real solution. You know this. You know the person in the kitchen will learn sooner or later, but the mess and the perceived errors are hard for you to take. That is exactly the same thing that is happening inside you. When you are able to stay in that discomfort and that pain, the mind is really defeated by that knowing. It is a really big disappointment.

The first step is to allow the discomfort; this will let you *be* more. The second step is to like it a little. The third step is to like it even more. And the fourth step is to accept it as okay and to know it's all right. That little clarity and that little knowing are all that you need to trust. Don't put any ointment on that discomfort. Don't convince yourself in any way. The discomfort is much better than being comfortable.

When I am in the discomfort, I can see it very easily, and at the same time my mind is saying, "I can do something about it to make it feel better."

And in the midst of both, what do you know?

Stay grounded in what I know.

With gentle okayness in the discomfort and gentle laying of the head from your mind It is like a little child who cannot do much; she only has the ability to stay in that place of doing a little bit, and yet this little bit is actually *not* little. This is a real eye-opener. It only feels little because there is nothing to do.

As there is discomfort, recognize the discomfort so you can be in it, rather than allowing the discomfort to overcome you. Don't try to *convince* yourself that you are okay. Can you see the difference?

Yes. With convincing there is a lot of pressure, and without the convincing, it just is.

Yes. If you convince yourself, then it is like lying to yourself, in a way. It doesn't matter what it is or in what amount it is present; just stay gentle with it. As you are gentle, give lots of room to the pressure. The pressure only feels like pressure when there is narrowness, and then there won't be enough room. When you are sitting at the kitchen table in that discomfort, you also feel powerless because you can't do anything about it and you have to watch. You previously had power, and in the power you were able to move everything quickly, but to be in the powerlessness is totally disappointing. However, inside, you do know something; you do know it is *you* feeling this internal struggle. The other person will learn sooner or later. And as you see all of this happening in you, it really, really brings in that tender shame within you.

You now know more, and that is melting you. You wanted to melt before, but you weren't able to. You wanted to be small before, but you weren't able to be small because you were thinking and believing differently from what you know the truth to be. The more you don't mind the tender shame, the more the shame is able to take you deep within. When you become more and more comfortable in it and realize you don't need to fix anything, then you come to understand that you don't need to be hard on yourself. It is not the doing; it's a result of what you are *being* in. Now you know more. That pain is much better; being hard on yourself isn't. When you are hard on yourself, you don't see that you are busy participating in it. In the heart you are able to see and feel because you are in the pain with your own permission. Do you see what this tenderness is doing to you?

I didn't think I could ever sit for this long with my hands tied and my eyes wide open—sitting calmly in the bottom of my heart and not doing anything with my hands.

So you are tasting the first restfulness within you.

145

Be in the Longing
and Not the Wanting

Sitting here in front of you, you touch me in such a way that I see my purity and I see my truth. It is real. But when I am engaged with my surface interactions in the world, I don't see that. Instead I seem shallow.

Be in the desperation to enter that shallowness in you.

I don't know how.

Be in and embrace that shallowness in you. When you don't embrace your shallowness, you are pushing it away, and pushing it away doesn't solve anything; it just causes more problems for you. Recognize that your hands are pushing and that they are busy. Being in your shallowness is not tasty; it's extremely bitter to you. But you must be willing to swallow that bitterness. The realness is within you; you know this, and you are the one who is covering it up.

So when I see myself in the unreal shallowness, am I to see and embrace it, and then will it take me to realness?

No, because if your eye is on results, then the shallowness won't take you anywhere. It's like you are bribing yourself. See your shallowness, and recognize that it is important to see and actually is real for you to be in it. You know that pushing it away doesn't work. Whatever is honest for you to be in, step in without looking for any kind of result; even if you want and need to have a result, or any kind of self-gain, just observe it. Observe it even when you are not in it. You cannot fight with your person in any way. If you fight with anything, you will create a monster. Simply lay your head down in every way with awareness.

Even the nectar you taste right now—don't let that taste go anywhere. But when you taste the nectar, don't go into wanting the nectar. Simply be happy that you are able to taste it. The tasting increases the longing in you. Be in the longing instead of the wanting. The longing will make you love it more. When you are in love with and are in pure longing, there is no such thing as wanting. Being in love will bring more readiness in you. The purity of being in love increases the capacity in you to the point where the cost doesn't matter anymore. When you are in love, everything you do will come through love. Then you don't lose yourself, because you can't separate your love from you. As you start *being* in love with this little bit of nectar, then you continue to be in love regardless of everything else, day and night. Then you become that love.

More Longing

Your presence is very strong, and I am so grateful to be here to have this experience. I want to be one with my real self. I can see where I love myself, and I can see where I do not.

Be in the dearness of that little bit of recognition that there is something happening within you. When you are in the dearness, it will actually fire up your longing for more.

This longing is not strong enough to get me where I want to be.

This longing brought you here, to a new beginning, and your longing needs to fire up more, because in this new beginning there will be much cost. And what is the cost? Everything you are holding on to mentally and emotionally needs to go. That is a big cost to the person.

So the things I hold on to, such as my patterns, have to go, and my person is afraid to let them go?

Even though you *try* to let go of your patterns, the person at the same time doesn't want to. That letting go is actually beyond your mind understanding. Even when you try at the surface to get rid of it, they won't go that way, and it won't work that way. What does work is recognizing in your heart that this is what you are holding on to—not outside of you, but in you.

Recognize the patterns honestly and *be* in that "holding on to" without trying to get rid of them, in honest beingness. Honest beingness shows you the many ways you are holding on to patterns and beliefs. That clarity itself is a letting go. Don't do anything. You just need to become honest within, but when you become honest within, there is a cost. You will be able to see and recognize so much more in so many different ways that there is self-gain about what you are holding on to.

You are *trying* to get rid of the patterns because you want something from them. When you want something from them, it won't work, because you are being dishonest in your seeing. When you are being dishonest with what you see, then you will convince yourself that you are seeing and letting go, but deep inside you aren't. *Only* your honesty works. Honesty sees the dishonesty. Don't mind seeing the dishonesty completely. When you see your patterns and you try to get rid of them because they are driving you crazy, you won't be able to, because you are threatening them. You want to kill your patterns so that you can be free from them. At the surface you can do it, but deep inside they will come back into you again; it is just a matter of time.

There is a little crack in you where you know that you love yourself so much, but at the same time you don't. Enter the little crack where you see you love yourself, and at the same time see where you don't love yourself. With that, begin to embrace everything and begin to see how you are imbalanced in the love. In this process you can feel like you are not getting any better, and you can actually feel you are getting worse because you are returning back to your creations and your issues. That is how it costs. With that cost, you don't expect a return. Be open to see more in this seeing. That is honesty. You cannot afford to be so hard on yourself. You need to be soft. So dearly like to be in your heart, and bring everything in front of you to embrace, little by little.

Permission

I see that I am protecting myself and could lose giving you permission and trust.

When there is a true relationship and you honestly trust that, then there is no fear of losing it. It's only when your trust is shaken that the fear comes, and then your person gets tangled up in that. There isn't any personal gain in this relationship. True relationships have a flow of the wonderfulness—much freedom, loveliness, and trust, which will continue to increase.

I see that my weakness becomes my person's gain.

So then be *in* that weakness. Don't push your weakness aside. It's not something bad. You feel that way only because the label has been there for so long, and it will take time to fully be in it. Weaknesses only trouble you when you participate in them blindly.

Yes, I see that in the awareness the weakness is not that threatening, and it doesn't even leave marks.

Gently and openly invite that weakness into you, and then there will be no marks, and then you become that weakness and there is no separation. There is just a lovely landing without noise.

So there is a kind of deep okayness with every aspect of myself as is, the way I am. No part is a threat in any way. I can just be open to everything now.

That part you *are* seeing.

I'm seeing that basically I'm protecting myself from me though there is no protection required. It's me giving power to this by labeling it all as weakness.

Yes, it's you troubling you. Let your inner self giggle! As you stay in this softness, the landings will become quicker and lovelier. So be in that pull of having lovely landings. To be in that little pull is more precious than anything else. You are holding on to the leash because of fear. So stand in that knowing, and then you will be able to see when you are open. Then be open regardless.

Can you say a little more about this "being open"?

With everything you have created, you have also created fear, doubts, wants, and needs. When you open to see *you* and that it's only been you who created this, just continue to keep seeing, because it doesn't end in just one glimpse. The doubt is still going to come even though you have already recognized it. The deeper you go, the trickier it is going to become, but stay open in what you know is true for you to be. Stay in that pull. When you open, you don't need to label anything. Just love opening up, and love moving through all that is inside of you and outside of you.

What is happening to me now?

You are opening up without fear and without judgment.

I feel I'm willingly going into quicksand.

Now you are trusting your love.

This is a beautiful feeling of hands free.

No hands, no feet, and the beauty is awesome.

And it's all around, inside and outside. I have always wanted to learn this way. This is amazement in itself.

And this amazement never ends, so give yourself in this amazement. Be in such softness that you don't go into wanting or needing this amazement. In this amazement, stay without your hands and feet. You are more natural, more real, and lovelier. That is the taste of it; the glimpse of it.

I'm so grateful. I just love this glimpse.

Even though it's a glimpse that is happening in you and you taste it, that glimpse is going to invite the rest of you in as you value it more. This is happening in you because you are giving permission.

No, it's all you. You are doing it all, even the permission—everything.

Because it is happening in me and you like it. As you give permission for this to happen, then it also happens in you. It's happening in me because I give the permission, and the permission continues growing. I enter that limitlessness so that you can join. You have joined by giving the permission. There is no limit, there is no time, and there is no color and no change of weather. It is amazing, and it is rich. It has all the wonderful qualities, all the grace. It has no form, yet it takes form and then goes back into formlessness. Only the ones who are ready will experience this. It is natural. This is soundless, and it is tasteless, yet it's rich.

It's like it's everlasting awe.

And it doesn't interfere, and yet it gives so much. It gives because that is the law of nature. That giving is not interfering, and it is beyond the mind's understanding of everything. The heart knows that only an awakened mind can see and be in it.

My mind is numb, but at the same time I feel something that I don't understand.

Because you can't understand, yet you *do* know something is happening. It's just that you haven't earned the full capacity yet.

But I'm feeling so much liking toward it.

Because that is the truth.

It's like a "wow" everywhere.

It is worth being in it and worth losing everything else.

It's as if the whole of creation has gone into your eyes and they are my windows. I feel as if my heartbeat is going to stop any second.

Because it is.

There is so much pull in that. It's like it's pulling me into it.

It's inviting you because you are opening your door. There is no cost; only for the person there is a cost. It's natural in the beginning, and it's natural at the end.

It is rich. Even this glimpse is worth everything.

Yes. If you are able to die in it, you will live in it.

Only after seeing the truth can one really see there is no value in the unreal. This is what you have shown me. I can't see unreal anywhere at all.

It's all being absorbed because everything needs to be absorbed within. You earn this by absorbing everything. Willingly open the doors to the parts that are untrue and are being labeled as bad. Everything needs to be absorbed in order to be one. First your feet enter, and then you give your heart, and then you give your mind. There is only purity, needing nothing and wanting nothing regardless of how lovely it is and regardless of how lost you are in it. Always stay in such smallness at every level without wanting any results.

It is taking precedence at every level, physical and mental.

You are not going to be the same after this—not the way you understand.

The only thing I know is that there is such a magnetic pull, such a magnetic attraction. There is something in your eyes; I can't even pull myself away.

You are open; it's being poured in.

Like an ocean—it's like an ocean of all qualities: grace, kindness, so much compassion and love. It's to die for.

This dying comes first in everything.

Honesty and Dishonesty

I am wondering what you mean by "honesty" and "dishonesty."

What I mean is seeing the honesty and dishonesty *within* you. Most people are not aware of their inner self, so when they are in the outside world, they think they are honest in their outer actions or reactions. This applies to everything—liking and disliking, loving and hating.

You must be completely honest about yourself, your desires, your wants, your needs, your beliefs, and your habits. If you are not honest with these things, you are not seeing what's inside you. So to be honest is to totally come back into *you* first. This means you can no longer blame others or focus your thoughts on judging others. The arrow must completely come into you first, and it must always stay there for you to see how honest you are being with yourself. The little bit of honesty will show you how dishonest you are with yourself. This is a challenge, because if you are honest with yourself, then you know the world you have created is not going to stay the same. This is why people stay busy outside themselves, thinking and believing "I am honest" in the surface world. But that has nothing to do with honesty. First, see you and only you. (Turn the arrow toward yourself and see your motivations and actions with honesty.) Seeing your own dishonesty is heartbreaking when you realize you have not been fair with yourself. You have tried to be fair with others, but you totally block your honesty to yourself. When you are thinking you are fair with others, it's just your created self doing that, not the real self.

As you grow to like being honest with yourself, you will find that the only thing you're going to see at this point is how dishonest you are with yourself and thus have been with others also. This has happened because you think you can serve others better, but in truth, it is just the opposite. If you are dishonest within yourself, you cannot serve honesty at all, but you cannot see this all at once. The person gives permission little by little to see its own dishonesty and its true self.

Before becoming aware of this, it was easy to blame others. It was easy because you didn't want to see that you were responsible for it. It is easy to stay weak and blind. Waking up is a very big responsibility. It shatters both worlds—inside your own world and outside your created world.

I concern myself quite a lot with others and their actions, reactions, and needs. I try to keep everything calm in my environment.

It is not about others at all; it is all about you. So come back into you and discover you. Every time your arrow goes toward other people, come back into you. It does feel more comfortable to have the arrow toward others, despite the hundreds or thousands of times you suffered because of this. But you decide for you.

At first keeping the arrow toward you is very uncomfortable, because it is totally opposite of what you are used to. But you *do* know what is real for you to be in. It's not other people; it's just your own patterns working. When you decide that you want to be honest, at any cost, then you will stand straight in that. That will be an honest decision. How you stand in it and how you walk in it matters. In this, you do feel like running away from it, because it feels uncomfortable.

When you are dishonest with yourself so that others stay calm, you are not doing any favors to them or to yourself. When you are honest, you know that it's not always a good feeling and that it may not be a good feeling for others either, but their hearts are much happier with the honesty than with the dishonesty. At the surface they may react, but that does not mean anything. You know deep inside what is true, and this is more meaningful.

Remember that honesty has more value. It does not matter what the outside picture looks like. What really matters is the little truth within you that chooses honesty, knowing it is more valuable. See what your heart is longing for and what your soul is longing for. Open up toward yourself.

It seems that honesty and dishonesty are tied up with patterns. How are patterns created?

People create these patterns themselves. You are able to see other people's patterns very easily, and they are able to see yours very easily. The patterns are so mechanical and so fast because the person creating them is sleeping. Because the person is sleeping, this allows the patterns to take over, and then the patterns are running the person, instead of the person being in charge of himself or herself. And now, because the person has been doing this for a long time, the person doesn't see the thickness and the blindness and how asleep he or she is. That is why honesty is so important. Honesty is able to see the patterns. Honesty likes to wake up. Honesty does not mind discomfort. Honesty does not mind the cost. Be desperate to see your own dishonesty at any cost. It will show you all the patterns in you, one by one. Stay firm in this. This may not be a very exciting way, but this is the real way. It can be very boring. It can be very heartbreaking, this path to reality, honesty, and the truth.

It seems that you are talking about the real humanness.

First look at the unreal humanness: managing, *trying* to manage, *trying* to be a good human being—all the different kinds of trying. But the person never becomes a real human being because of the dishonesty. That little drop of honesty in you—love this; it's bringing you back to this. Value that drop in you; it's most precious.

Being in Discomfort

Sometimes I'm in my heart and it feels effortless and restful, and other times there is a lot of discomfort.

Learn to be in that discomfort, because you do satisfy yourself too easily. Remember and be in the flash of discomfort that you experience. Long to be in your discomfort all the time. Being in discomfort will help you to open up more. And in that beingness, you won't feel openness; you will just feel discomfort. You have a habit of satisfying yourself too easily.

I know that, and I see when I am doing that.

Be in the discomfort all the time, and be comfortable in your discomfort all the time. Being in that kind of discomfort does not mean you are closing your door; it just means you need to be in it all the time. Stay in that narrowness. When you stay in it, you won't know what is next. Let yourself expand in the discomfort day and night. Being in discomfort means you don't have to worry about any mistakes, because you don't have to be perfect. Being in discomfort, comfortably, is expanding you at the same time; it is a lot to be in.

I'm not sure how to stay in the discomfort.

Be desperate. Be desperate enough to keep the discomfort in you by keeping your face turned toward it whenever you taste it inside you. It's like when you're used to living in a small room that is easy to take care of; when you expand that room, the discomfort multiplies because the room becomes more of a responsibility. As soon as you leave parts of the room empty, you are letting the walls come closer to you again. Discomfort is a help. Give more room to the discomfort in every moment. When you *be* in the discomfort, then you can easily see how you are not okay, instead of convincing yourself that you *are* okay.

I want to do this properly; I guess I am a perfectionist.

No perfection. Perfection easily takes you to your mind. Instead, don't mind the imperfections. You're just fine when you're not okay with imperfection. Let your *not* being okay expand you. Allow yourself to experience the discomfort in you about not being okay. That way you become naked, which lets your secrets appear in front of you. You will never believe you have those secrets otherwise. Live from your fineness so that you can let those moments come in when you're not okay. Being in the discomfort will slowly show you feelings of not being okay. First learn to be in your discomfort and let the discomfort open you up a little more. Even the tiniest little bit of not being okay is enough for you to enter. Convincing yourself creates a shell, and there is a comfort in that shell. But eventually that shell will create discomfort also. Being in this *new way* takes a lot of responsibility.

Embracing Our Temptations

I have some repeated temptations, and these temptations keep me from my heart, and I feel shame. I am exhausted from struggling with them.

When you feel that your temptations are bad and you have that feeling of shame, this prevents you from being in those feelings in a direct way. Remove every judgment and all your beliefs about these temptations. That will let you see them in a direct way. The more you relate to them directly, the more you will simply see there is no truth in them. When you see there is no truth in something, slowly and in a friendly way just learn to stay closer to it in a direct way. In this directness you are not bending, not labeling, and not trying to convince yourself differently. This way you delicately move closer to your temptations.

Use what comes up in the outside world to show you your temptations, and then enter them. This is a very delicate process; you cannot disturb any water around them. You must be kind, still, and honest that you are not going to try to change anything. You only need to enter them. Any temptation you threaten will make you harden, and then you are being dishonest. You can't enter them in this way. You need nothing from your temptations, and there is nothing there for you.

You can be awakened in your temptations from inside. When you awaken inside in a temptation, that will let you see how you have been playing with them or are being driven by them. Enter, and if the experience touches your feelings and your emotions, that's okay; and if it touches your disappointments, disheartened feelings, and your sadness, that's okay too. Stay with that honest choice where you just love to enter it. There isn't one level in awakening; you will continually awaken by entering into everything inside you. You earn more and more awareness as you go within. That love is your drive. It will encourage you.

When you are driven by temptations, and when you become aware of this each time, you may feel guilt, and you may feel shame, but know there is no truth in that. In this way, you accumulate guilt. Even if there is guilt, it won't be something bad now, because now you love to wake up and you know the value of waking up. When you know the value of waking up, you don't mind the pain, the guilt, or the shame; these are all welcome. Continue to open your heart to everything in whatever way things come up, with no judgment. Continue to open your doors to everything, whether there is shame, guilt, or pain. Then you are allowing everything to rest in you. The more you let it rest inside, the more you will earn love in you. You might not feel what you earn, but you know. You just know.

Waking up helps the rose to continually flower. The person always gives preference to what feels good. Awakening is not always pleasant, because the created self is always looking for the good feelings. However, awakening is truth. Keep trusting this awakening step-by-step. It will open you up from inside. As you learn and as you walk, be comfortable with whatever is opening up inside you. That is how you learn to give lots of room inside to everything, in a simple way. When you give room, then you don't make anything big. Remember, when you make something big, you block the flow, and then it becomes overwhelming.

Diminishing Beliefs

I had a dream about big waves smashing me and a monster that was coming to get me. I was in great fear.

Little by little, let yourself be comfortable in the fear in order to see what you are afraid to see. Whatever you are afraid to see, don't make a story about it. When you believe the story, that won't let you see the reality, because believing the story gives form to it. When you give form to it, that itself protects you from facing the reality. Your restfulness lets you see.

How can I let myself rest?

By giving no energy to your beliefs, regardless of how dear the beliefs are.

If beliefs come, what should I do?

Whatever belief system comes, you need to see it and let it diminish back into you. That can scare you in the beginning, but trust that first little bit so that you can put your foot in where you allow your beliefs to diminish little by little.

Lately I am doing things that are against my beliefs, and it's very uncomfortable.

Instead of going against your beliefs, let yourself see that it is *you* that has these beliefs. At first that will make you uncomfortable, but learn to be okay in your beliefs, and let them slowly diminish in you by seeing that they are only beliefs.

So see the beliefs, observe them, and let the intensity of the feeling diminish?

When you observe your beliefs, you are still keeping a distance from them. When you see them, be *in* them. Slowly let these beliefs in you diminish. As you *be* and become more restful, let yourself see these beliefs comfortably and allow the beliefs to diminish. Your person is not going to like it. Regardless of your dislike, give preference to the reality and value waking up in every way.

The beliefs seem very close to me, and it's hard for me to see them.

Yes, but at the same time you *are* seeing, because you are talking about your beliefs. When you begin to see your beliefs with honesty, this helps you to see the next one and then the next one. In seeing them, it does feel too big. In the beginning it will seem very big and scary. That's what you are seeing through your dream of the waves that threaten to smash you. This seeing means you have given permission to yourself. Still you need to learn to be in the restfulness. Being in restfulness helps you see the real way. There is nothing scary about the real way.

Tell me again how I can be in restfulness.

When you are aware of a belief, keep it in front of you and just let yourself see it as is instead of trying to put form to it.

I feel I am in the dark right now.

What is the darkness doing to you?

It's comfortable; I like it, and I welcome it. I'm not afraid of it now.

Then let yourself land in the darkness in every way. Letting yourself land in the darkness is your first step in being honest toward losing what you see. Just be in that simple knowing that it's okay to be in the darkness. Continue to let yourself land by giving permission to this all the time. Be in the darkness in such a simple way. Lose all your hope for the light; lose it and *like* going deeper into the darkness.

I feel as if I'm inside the monster in the water and I'm just walking inside it.

Yes, that's how you are going deeper into the darkness without making anything up about it. Walk in the darkness, and at the same time stay open to see. Walk in a simple way, not convincing yourself about anything.

In your presence, this walking is so easy, with no fear, no pressure—just walking. I'm so touched. It seems layers of fears and resistance have just dropped.

If you continue to walk in the darkness, that little bit of knowing will slowly appear in a very simple way. In that knowing you will see that what you are hanging on to has been created by you.

Feeling Lost and Empty

I'm really lost in life, and I need help.

Since you know you feel lost, *be* in that lost feeling from your side with awareness. If you continue to participate in the lost feelings, then you are actually getting more lost. In being tangled up in feeling lost, you keep *saying* it, but you're not *being* in it.

I don't know the difference between participating in the lost feelings and standing by while watching the lost feelings.

See the difference. When you keep *saying* that you are lost, you then see that you are not *being* in it and are participating in the feelings. It's as though you keep running away from your home. The louder you speak about it, the further you drift away from home. Just *be* and let yourself *see* your lostness with awareness in a restful way. Your mental body is not going to solve any of your problems. As you come back inside of you, be in that lostness with awareness, as that will slowly help you to recognize *you*.

Allow yourself to unfold in your lost feelings, and then you will be able to see *you*. See how you are creating the lost feelings and not *being* in the lost feelings. In beingness (heart) you will not find intellectual answers. You are looking for answers, but none of the intellectual answers will solve your problem.

Yes, I try to do everything mentally and intellectually.

This habit increases your feelings of being lost. Being outside of yourself won't let you open your eyes, but returning back into your heart *will* open your eyes.

So I need to learn how to be in the lostness?

Yes. For you it's easy to talk but hard for you to *be*. Beingness is your responsibility. In repeating "I am lost," you are irresponsible and you are not grounded.

By "lost" I mean an existential emptiness.

You're not connecting within you to the meaningfulness. Meaninglessness is like you have no ground that is your own. You are already seeing that, and you know how you're feeling about it, but don't run away from those feelings and those disappointments. Every disappointment, every disheartened feeling, is worth being in. Be awake in it. Let these things land in you, and then you will connect with meaningfulness for you. When you are kind and aware, that is the type of life you will live—a kind and aware life. Your feelings of meaninglessness are not the result of anything outside being wrong. Use every disheartened feeling within you to become awakened.

Connect with your disappointments in you instead of trying to avoid them. Instead of being nowhere, you are somewhere; you are back in you. When your mental body tries to take you away, instead of participating and trying, just come back into you. Being in your disappointments may slowly take you to your emptiness. That's okay. Learn to *be* in that emptiness.

I'm saying this because you will be moving away from the noise, which brings about uncomfortable feelings, but continue to choose to be in it and make it worthwhile. Then you will slowly learn to trust in *you* instead of in your thinking. You know that you're missing trust in yourself, so do everything to be in your feeling of being lost and disappointed. It's perfectly okay if nothing changes; just trust being in it. That tiny baby step shows you the next step.

This is all just showing you how much you are staying in the shallow because you keep looking for a cure. Instead of looking for a cure, be forever in the lostness as though you don't need any cure at all. That is the tiny trust you will earn back in you. Trust is not something that will come from outside of you. You *earn* trust by being what you see in you.

When you don't trust what you feel, you open too many doors at the surface and confuse yourself. Learn to be in it from your side instead of confusing yourself through opening so many doors at the surface. Just trust a little bit; it will help you to go in one direction—inward.

Okay, I need to learn how to go inward, but I don't know how to start doing that.

Stop participating by expecting answers from the outside—from me or from anywhere. *Be* what you are inside.

Being a Loner

I feel like I am becoming somewhat of a loner; I don't feel like talking to anyone much anymore.

You are losing familiarity, which is creating discomfort in you. Keep your head down, and as your head is down, walk with trust.

I find my love and trust for you growing. Even in all the chaos and loneliness, my love is growing more and more. I sometimes even see that love is growing toward myself.

When you participate in discomfort, recognize it, and as you recognize it, be in it. You will give power to anything you participate in. So don't participate; just recognize it and *be* in it.

I recognize my discomfort, but you say not to participate in the discomfort. I don't understand the difference between recognizing it and being in it.

When you are uncomfortable in whatever issue is happening around you at that moment, you are unknowingly participating in the discomfort blindly. Being in the discomfort with more and more clarity (seeing the discomfort) will continue to open you up more. As you are being in the discomfort with clarity, you are moving closer to yourself; previously, the discomfort was keeping you at a distance. As you cleanly *be* in the discomfort, then you will become that. Each time you enter a new door, the entry shows you more. In the awareness that you want to be a loner, you do know the truth of it. It is the person that is making a little bit of a fuss because it is losing its familiarity. Embrace being a loner.

I am embracing the aloneness and seem to be walking through another door.

Then read the welcome sign. This is another entrance that you are able to walk through comfortably in your aloneness. As you enter such a beautiful opening, everything becomes much easier for you. Be in this embracing, and with each embrace, include everything as you see it.

Being Shattered

An event has shattered my heart. I tried to be in that shattered, mourning place. I sat with my shattered heart and was surprised as to how sweet pain really can be. It is like sugar. I realized that it is a raw, vulnerable place to be.

Through these shattered feelings, and as you become softened, you can feel the touch of that sweetness of your pain. Value that sweetness of this dear pain, and then you will slowly learn that it is not about being happy at the surface. It's not about just good feelings inside you. It is about what keeps you closer to yourself.

Knowing what keeps you closer to yourself will give you new eyes. Then, instead of feeling too up and down, you will find the smoothness where you simply know. In that knowing, you know it is not about happiness. Any feeling, regardless of how good you feel about it, is always temporary. When you know that it is temporary, don't easily satisfy yourself there. Otherwise, you might lose yourself. That is what creates the sleepiness and ignorance toward yourself. It is about being awakened in everything that is temporary in you. As you have already tasted these feelings of being shattered and how much you are aware of yourself in this, bring the same awareness into your happy times.

I actually liked being in that pain and stayed in it with no desire to change it. I was really proud of myself, because I usually run from pain as fast as I can run. I am getting better and better with pain.

Even in your happy times, kindly stay grounded, very kind, and very okay. Every bit is helping you to be. When you let everything help you to *be,* then there is nothing wrong in anything. Just gracefully move through everything. Your openness, your kindness, and your okayness let you move through everything in such a dear way. Stay aware in your happiness and your sadness. Remember, give yourself in the same way to both, where nothing is personal.

What does that mean, "where nothing is personal"?

It means that you don't own the happiness. When you don't own the happiness, you will do the same thing with the sadness. Inside of you, when you really feel good, you can easily become blind in it. When you are blind in your happiness, then the opposite side, which is sadness, is right beside you, and then you can easily fall in it. So always stay grounded whenever you have happy feelings. Being grounded will slowly bring clarity to you. It is only when you are not grounded that you don't have clarity, because by not being grounded you are actually participating in it.

I can see that.

You will become one with anything that you are participating with, and you can't see it when this happens. Do this seeing in a kind way. It is not that participating is something bad; it is just something valuable that you now know.

It's a huge key for me.

Yes, and when you decide to open the door with that key, keep opening all the doors, and that will take you beyond your emotions and feelings, where there is nothing personal. When there is nothing personal, just move through with everything as it is. Being in your feelings and emotions unfolds much of the person. In the unfolding, learn to stay grounded in every way and learn to trust in every way. Because of the familiarity in the beginning, it is a little difficult to start. It is difficult because you are losing what is familiar to you.

I am ready to lose. Finally ready to lose.

Then stay closer to this permission. When you stay closer to this permission, it will help you to move through the difficulties. It will let you move through the distrust and then allow you to lose.

I know that I am losing things of very little value.

Even lose what you *do* value. Just let yourself see.

I know that those things I value are not valuable.

In letting yourself see, don't put anything to the side. Let everything come in front of you in order to move through it.

I knew the shattering I was feeling was necessary for me to come alive and wake up.

You just use every bit of it without being hard on yourself.

I really see clearly that this journey has nothing to do with anyone else. That is why I am so grateful that I have this sight now.

That is a nice golden key you have received.

I feel so lucky to have woken up to that. It's a beautiful golden key that I will cherish and keep with me. I won't forget.

In every way, be very kind to yourself. Whether you are clear with yourself or you are not, you need all the kindness.

I feel as if I am melting like toffee. Everything in my body is melting.

Stay with every little touch you have in a very delicate way. The way you are being softened will change you, instead of you trying to change yourself. Continue to value this softness in you in every way.

It feels so much better to be soft. It feels like being home, and it's a relief not to have to protect. I see a little girl. She is sweet and soft, and she is smiling at me. I think she may be my inner child.

Then you know what doesn't let her live.

Yes. Protection.

Forgiving Myself and Others

How do I begin the process of forgiving?

So you see that you're holding on to something in you. In a very soft way, be soft with it instead of trying to get rid of it. Right now even though you know you're holding on to it, you aren't staying in it. Choose to stay in it with the softness until you become that softness in you. When you make an honest decision to see that you are holding on to something (anger, fear, jealously, or resentment, for example), you must stay in those emotions all the time. And you must do so not only because you want to forgive yourself, because that is just a beginning. Honest decisions won't let you satisfy yourself in the surface world. Stay in the decision so you can learn to *be* in a *true way* forever. By standing in this honest decision, you live for the deepest in you. By living for the deepest, you open your doors and let everything in, little by little. When you stand firm in your decision, you will slowly build a stronger backbone, and that way you won't bend in front of your weaknesses. Just openly let your weaknesses diminish in you. Weaknesses are not bigger than you. Unknowingly you have given them power, and they are unknowingly preventing you from waking up. Wake up in your honesty. Waking up is the good news your real self wants to hear.

I really want to find forgiveness for all the people in my life and for myself.

Your experiences are showing you where you are going. You are still moving through your emotional and intuitional layers. Every layer will keep you separate from yourself even when you think that you are forgiving people. Instead of thinking about forgiving others and yourself, just *be* in that forgiveness. Then forgiveness will not be a doing. Forgiveness is not something you do once and then are done with. By being with an honest heart forever, each layer is cleared as you move within.

The step you are taking now is showing you how to *be* a little bit. Be you in an honest way. Don't sacrifice anything. You are standing in what you know the truth to be. By standing in what you know the truth to be, then little by little you cause what you thought was a sacrifice to shatter, because that is only a belief.

As you come back inside of you to the aloneness, you know it is true. But the old self still does its best to try to disturb you. With every disturbance, you learn more. In the learning, always stay with the true choice you have made in a very kind way. Keep coming back inside you. Because you have a strong emotional body, that emotional body is easily able to manipulate you. Learn to stay calm in your emotions, and then you will be able to learn the little tricks you get wrapped up in. By recognizing the tricks, little by little, you will be awakened in your emotional body, where you are able to see with clarity. That recognition will bring you a little bit closer to you, and by coming back closer, you will feel the lessness that is a little bit of nothingness. By being in lessness, you will be able to enter you, and nothingness will be unlimited in you. Remove your trying hands and embrace the nothingness with your heart in a gentle way.

I feel so peaceful right now.

This is because you are touching your deep. Always receive the unexpected guests in you in the same way you are experiencing it now. Don't run away from the pain; look for the pain so that you can embrace it deeply.

Embracing Negativity

I find myself going into old patterns. The pattern is to go to the dark side of things and find things wrong. I catch myself, and I say I shouldn't be that way.

Which way shouldn't you be? You said, "I shouldn't be that way."

I find negativity in everything rather than seeing the goodness.

Give me an example.

Phoning someone and talking for hours about how bad things are or how I don't have this or that. It's much easier for me to find something negative or dark to talk about.

There is nothing wrong with the darkness or negativity. The issue is that you are participating in it, and when you participate in those thoughts, you blind yourself. When you do participate in it, you wish the negativity would go away and want goodness.

Sometimes I can't see any goodness at all.

You can't see goodness because you are in the negativity and participating in it, and you are labeling something really bad. You won't accept anything that you think is bad. You say, "No, no, go away." When you participate in it, you keep increasing the intensity and then you continue to fight it. You continue to participate because you wish you didn't participate. But when you participate, you totally blind yourself in order to participate. Instead of blinding yourself, be okay in seeing that pattern that you have. You label the pattern as very big and bad. The bigger the label, the more you don't want to see it, because in your mind it is an extremely negative thing to be seeing. If you remove the label and trust yourself to be in that pattern, then that pattern won't drive you. You will be able to see it beforehand.

In the beginning, be in the pattern a little bit here and there. The more desperate you are to be in that pattern, the easier it will be for you to be in that pattern. It just needs your permission. You are the one scaring that pattern, and you are the one who is able to give the permission to see that pattern. When you give the permission to be in that pattern and you dial the number to your friend to talk about all the bad things that are happening to you, you won't be able to keep the conversation going that way for too long, because you will see that pattern.

You are only able to see the pattern when you are in the pattern and you see that you are participating in it. Participating will continue to subside because you won't be giving as much energy to it in the way you were participating before. *Like* being in the desperation so you can be in that pattern.

Are you saying that with my awareness of this pattern, I can stop it?

You can't stop it even if you want to. You could say, "I'm not going to participate in it; I'm not going to phone my friend and talk about it anymore." If you do this, you will secretly repeat the same pattern, but in different ways. You can't stop the pattern unless you have honestly seen what is driving the pattern. Go into the root of the pattern, and it will bring a lot of honesty until there is no self-gain underneath. If there is self-gain, even the deep desire to be free from that pattern won't work. It just depends on how honest you are in that.

You know there is a pattern, and you know that this pattern is driving you because the results do not feel good. But you haven't actually been in the pattern yet; it's something at a distance. If you give the permission that it is okay and that you'd like to be in the pattern, the pattern will come to you because you are opening the door for the pattern so you can be in it. It is a *true way* to be.

I have a lot of judgment about this.

Then just take a gentle look. It's just that you label everything too big. You are learning this.

I guess it is what I've done for a long time.

But it is okay that you are *not* okay in it. Ask yourself, "Why do I have a judgment? Why am I negative? Why am I not good?" You continue to beat yourself up. As you begin to see that you are *not* good enough, gently be in that seeing and stay in that seeing without hoping that it goes away. Just know that you are as you are and that you don't need to change anything. It is *you* not being okay with the negativity that keeps troubling you. You keep beating yourself up for no reason. As you accept and continue to embrace the way you are, then it will become okay.

When you are not okay and you want to be different, you keep going in circles. You must *like* to embrace whatever you presently are and what you are presently seeing, even if it brings discomfort and even if all you want to do is embrace the goodness and ignore the negative. All the goodness is underneath that which you are not embracing. If someone gives you a glass of negativity and the person is holding another glass of goodness, which one would you drink? Would you drink the negative one first?

Yes.

Then do. Happily do so. Drinking the negativity is a big favor to you. It doesn't matter what it tastes like.

I need to be kind to myself. This seems so hard.

Gently embrace the unkindness in you. Embracing the unkindness *is* a kindness. Regardless of how much unkindness you have, never feel tired of embracing it. In the past you worked so hard to build that wall bigger and bigger. When you build a wall that says you have to be a good person and then all of a sudden you realize you don't need that wall, it is such a relief to you. It's such a relief that you don't have to be a good person, that you are just okay as you are now. Then there will be nothing to do. Isn't that a big relief?

I wish I could just accept what you are saying. Right now I have so many judgments about myself.

Be okay in it and accept yourself. When you are not okay, you continue to fight with yourself, and in the fight, you never win. The pattern gets stronger and stronger because you keep fighting with the person. It doesn't feel right to stop fighting, because it is totally opposite of what you have been taught. *Doing* something seems to feel right. When you do something, you say to yourself, "I am getting better, and I am doing something to get better." When you suddenly drop this behavior, you say to yourself, "I don't need to do anything; the way I am is okay now." You begin to see that you have been pushing the pattern away, and that's okay. When you see this, the pattern will come back into you slowly. Everything has to go back into you—everything that you have been pushing away. Whether it is pain, shame, negativity, or all your wants and needs, embrace everything, and it will all diminish in you.

Can you remember how the negativity was born in you? Where did this negativity come from in the first place? It came from you, did it not? So then it has to go back into you in order to be the end of it.

Are you saying that I believed what people said and took that on? Is that what you are saying?

Be in it openly without participating in it. When someone is talking to you and you think it is negative and you think it is hurting you, that is when you close your door. You say to yourself, "I don't want to take it. It's negative; it's bad." And then you put a lot of energy into it. Focusing on the problem uses a lot of energy and power to block it so that it doesn't go into you. You think it is the other person who has the pattern of doing this, but at the same time, you don't know you are doing it. This is not helping you. You think to yourself, "I'm better now; I've blocked it," but you know it is not working. It's just your fear that is holding it together, and the fear is not going to go anywhere. The negativity is not going to go anywhere; it is just waiting for you to open the door so it can enter. When you open the door, what happens?

I go into the pain.

It is much better than the struggle, because the struggle is not doing anything. You are just building more of this pattern, which is driving you crazy. You are just using your energy for nothing. Open your door and honestly see how much it hurts. The more it hurts, the better it is. Then you see how good the pain is and it doesn't hurt anymore. It only hurts because that is the way you have been thinking and believing about yourself. You do not need to cage yourself within the cage of "I don't like it because I know it is bad for me." When you are free from the cage, what is left?

Well, then I am free.

Then is it right for you or wrong for you? Would you rather live in the freedom of not protecting yourself or live in the cage of "I want to be good"?

I want freedom to be.

Then open your door to embrace without judgment and accept all the negativity, all the hurt, all the pain. That is real kindness when you embrace the way you are, step-by-step. Embracing brings the gentleness, the kindness, and the freedom. Embracing melts you and takes you deeper. Embracing shatters what you have believed. Embracing is the answer. It is the truth. Embracing has no judgment; no negativity. Just embrace, regardless of what it feels like, regardless of what it looks like, and regardless of what it tastes like.

Discontentment

I am not content anymore.

That is really good.

There is a great deal of pain and depth to this discontentment.

Love being in the pain of not being content. *Not* being content brings much more to you, so be comfortable as you are in that pain. The more you are comfortable in the pain, the more you give room to it and the more you will open up. That openness will show you there is a lot to integrate.

Now you are able to see that being content has kept you on the surface. The pain you feel now is really opening you up in a deep way. Willingly go into the pain as if you cannot escape or avoid it. Let this pain open you up, knowing that there will be a cost—your person. In any kind of contentment, a person is actually not happy. You think and believe that you are, but this is not reality. So keep this in front of you.

Trust the little bit of knowing underneath the pain, and use that same knowing to guide you deeper into the pain. Remember to do this gently, even though you are in pain. You don't need to be hard on yourself; otherwise, you will not be able to give any room to the pain. When you are in the pain and you gently allow the pain, your heart is much happier, even though the person may not feel good or happy. As you go deeper into your pain, you will be able to see that the heart doesn't mind any kind of pain; only the person does. Love to be comfortable with the way you are. Being comfortable as you are brings the realness in you.

Don't believe what you're thinking in the mind. You may think you are comfortable, but go deeper than that and actually apply the comfortableness within yourself. That's how you earn everything, by taking a little step within and then actually applying it.

Family Resistance

I talked about this before, but my husband doesn't want me to come here. Sometimes I have to miss sessions. I don't want to stop coming, but he doesn't like it.

You do know truth does cost. It does cost everything.

How can I handle this better?

Only you can take the pain.

I can do that; it's not a problem to take the pain.

Inside of him, he knows this too.

He is quite deep himself. I don't know why he is not coming. It's been two years since I started to come to see you. I know it's hard for him.

You are changed, and he does not like it. Whatever you used to feed him, you cannot do it anymore.

We've been together a long time.

Before you came here, you knew only the mind. This discord is caused by you actually moving forward. You cannot convince him in any way, and the more you try, the more he is going to go in the opposite direction. Just be in your heart and be kind to him and loving toward him as you move in this walk toward you.

I have a lot of respect for him; he is very nice in every way. But when he hears your name, he goes into resistance.

It's quite natural to the person, but what you have to learn is to stand straight.

The problem is, when I come here, the same thing happens every time.

So what is true for you? If you don't stand straight in what is true for you to be, then you are feeding your weakness. Don't focus on him; focus on you. Focus on your own weakness. When you focus on him, you also create trouble. Your fear of how he is going to react creates more chaos. That is why you have to focus on you. You will have to stand up for yourself and for this truth one day anyway. That you already know. He is showing you your weakness. If you focus on him, you will miss what the lesson is for you. If he didn't respond to you coming here, then you wouldn't see your weakness.

Every opportunity with your husband is showing you something in you, so use this opportunity. He is helping you in many ways for you to see you; he is helping you grow. But instead, you want *him* to see you. When you begin to honestly use his help to show you your weakness, you will see the change in you both. He is already showing you how much you are leaning on him, which you weren't seeing before.

No, I don't listen to him, but he always wants me to.

When you were feeding his person, you were also feeding *your* person. You weren't helping him, and at the same time you weren't helping yourself either. You have been leaning on your patterns for a long time, and you were allowing others to misuse you, and you were misusing others blindly. When you start having your backbone straight, it won't be like that anymore, but your person is not going to like it.

Does that mean I should let it happen? Whatever happens, just go with it?

Not in an irresponsible way; only in a responsible way inside you. See your weakness, but at the same time, be kind and loving in your heart toward others. It's not that you will take away the pain or that you don't have a problem. You can't bend truth, and what you know is true for you. Stand in that in every situation, step-by-step. When you are unconscious about yourself, you are able to feed your person and your husband in the same way. Then you are unconsciously feeding both of you, which will cause more and more suffering. You can't afford to be unconscious. You knew this before, but it was never in practice before. The more you learn about how you were feeding your own person and your own weakness, the more you will be able to see that what you were doing to him was never true. So in that reality and on the surface, it creates a lot of chaos, and yet underneath you do know what is happening.

Have a broader view about yourself and see a more comfortable way of being with yourself. When you learn how to stand straight in this, you can include him in your heart and walk straight in you and not in his person. Underneath the chaos, his heart knows, and the heart is always happy; it's just the person that is not happy.

Allow the pain of this chaos into your heart and stay with that simple pain; not the why, what, or how, but just the simple pain. Let the simple pain go deeply into your heart, and as your awareness continues, stay with that pure pain forever. You need not protect yourself, but give more room in the heart to that pain; comfortably and openly just embrace the pain with kindness.

What is it like now?

I feel pain.

So increase your awareness, because when you are not in awareness, you will go back into an old pattern. When you are wrapped up in your weakness, this is how you protect yourself from the pain, and you think, "I am able to take it." The way you are experiencing this pattern right now is that you are directly being in it.

Annoyance with Others

Some people annoy me, and it brings out the worst in me. I try to put the arrow toward myself, but I often think the annoyance is not my doing.

Other people's behavior is showing you to connect to what you don't like in yourself. What can you do now? It's you. You cannot run away from you.

So I need to learn to accept others?

Learn to *be* in it wholeheartedly even when it doesn't feel good. What you recognize in others is also in you; you didn't believe this before, but now you're beginning to face it. When you face what is in you completely, then you'll respect the person who helped you to see those things in you. In the beginning, when you start to see this, do your best to be in it without lifting your head up even a little bit. Be in that seeing wholeheartedly forever. That person is (wonderfully) showing you that what you were seeing in others is in you. Now live, in a most fire-full way, for what you see in you. When others show you what is inside of you, you don't need to mend anything at the surface; just let the acceptance come, fire-fully.

Self-Sabotage

One of my patterns is that my mind is always very busy, so I don't focus on what I should. I tend to become quiet and daydream, and then I panic that I didn't follow through with my commitments. I sabotage myself.

Every time you drift away, don't panic. Recognize your panic right away. Instead of participating in it (going blind in the panic), keep your hands off and just see the panic with awareness. Recognizing it quickly is important. When you participate, you know you are caught in it, and then you panic and you get caught in it further. It is okay. Stay in that discomfort.

Whether you're anxious about an issue or some form of negativity doesn't matter. Know that it is *okay*. That knowing and the use of more awareness will help you to catch it quicker. This reminder to be quicker than before can never be said enough. Never go after that quietness. Don't pursue it; simply enjoy the quietness. When you run after it, you want that period of quietness to last, but what happens is you lose track and the busyness comes back into you.

The track back into yourself can be right where you lost it, and if you are gentle with yourself, you can go back in the knowing again. The kinder you are with yourself, the more this will give you the ability to embrace the negativity that increases; then you won't make a big deal about it. The kindness shows you how hard you are on yourself, so stay in it kindly and stay in your feet. (Maintain humbleness.)

You don't need to curse yourself because you have bad patterns. The patterns aren't bad; it's just you being hard on yourself. The patterns are there to help you; they will take you inward into you. They are rooted in you. There is a pattern ladder that can take you deeper into you.

There is weariness about this, and it is exhausting. It takes a lot of effort.

Only because you are hard on yourself. It is as though you keep screaming, "I am very bad." You continue to make that label bigger and bigger, and yet you so badly want to be better. There isn't anything that says you need to be better or be nice. Be real when entering into the discomfort, and be in your feet, and like being in your feet. Instead of being busy fighting with the mind, be busy staying in the feet.

I have tears, and I am running away inside right now.

You have been running away from yourself and your past, but now you are coming back, so trust this without labeling the past; just enjoy the now. Anything you think is bad, gently *be* okay in it, but do not participate in it. Welcome everything in the present as you apply the kindness.

So just by honoring what is happening to me, that would be applying kindness? There's a voice that says it's going to be all right.

It's already all right; it's just that you don't believe it. Do you see that you are a little more kind to yourself right now? This little bit of kindness shows you how unkind you have been to yourself in the past because you were expecting something different. Bit by bit, trust.

So what do you trust the most in you?

I trust two things: putting my feet on the ground and going into my heart.

The okayness within you is so much more than before. Trust that, because you know.

Self-Doubt and
Judgment of Others

I judge others, and I also judge myself. I have so much self-doubt and doubt a lot of my decisions in life.

When people judge the outside world and others, they take on too much of a load from the outside world. In doing this, they unknowingly collect outside heaviness, though they have enough to deal with on the inside.

Keep the arrow pointed inward. Instead of having too many outward influences, keep coming back into the self and be responsible for your own actions. The mind becomes a monster in collecting garbage from the outside world by listening to gossip and making judgments about outside things.

Often I react in the moment, but after the event I am always aware that I should have responded in a different way. I often regret decisions I make because I react too quickly.

It is okay if you make mistakes in your decisions. Becoming aware of this after the fact is okay too. Just take responsibility and see how you can open up in it, and don't let the opportunity to *see* slip by. Bring it back into your awareness so you can take responsibility for your actions. This way you are not scattered. Whenever the self-doubt comes, be okay. When self-doubt is dropping, it will let you be what you are. Let it rest, and be very aware that you are being affected by self-doubt. As you grow in awareness, self-doubt can just go *its way,* and you will no longer be affected by it. Become simple.

You are not doubt, and doubt is not you. Don't keep rolling around in it; you tend to put yourself in a little hole of self-doubt. Ask the self-doubt, "What is there?" Go into the core, but rest from *trying* to fix it all; just ask yourself, "Why am I holding on to anything, and what is the point of holding on to anything?" There is a fear of moving forward. On one hand you want to move forward, and on the other hand you are feeding the self-doubt. Just be clear. What is there to lose?

I am involved in another spiritual group, and I get confused by the different spiritual teachings.

I do see people who have another spiritual focus as well as this one, and I see a little split inside of them. Just love this walk so your flow is undivided. You can't have two teachers. Sometimes when people come here they are still holding on to other belief systems. I often say to them, "The more you come, the more clarity you will have about all your baggage."

Be clear and solid in everything. Ask yourself over and over, "What am I going lose if I drop spirituality?" Some people come to talk to me and speak with so much knowledge about spiritual matters, but the words mean nothing, they are just programmed with the words they use. It's easy to get caught in that. But where I am, it is so simple. Fancy words, intellectual words, are indirect. This walk is direct.

I see I am involved with this other spiritual group because I am afraid to be alone.

Look at what you are afraid to face in you about being alone. Throw yourself in the aloneness; you don't have to wait any longer. Bring it into yourself. See what you are scared to lose. Is it your job, your money, your friends? Be willing to lose everything, including your money. Move through it all, and become empty. Yes, it is scary, but don't hold on to that fear. Just move through the fear. Bring it back into you, and lose it right now. Lose all the friends, lose your job, and lose all the spiritual beliefs. Just keep losing all of it.

Now, you have just lost everything in your whole world at this moment. Where are you? Who are you? You just lost everything. Don't think; *feel* that you have lost everything in this whole world. Everything is lost, so where you are? Are you still there?

Yes, I am.

You see, you never lost yourself, so stay in the lostness and in the aloneness, naked. It is okay. As soon as a thought comes, just say to it, "I don't need that." It doesn't matter if it is a pleasant or unpleasant thought; just stay empty and alone. Choose to stay alone; there is nothing wrong with that.

Don't get involved in too many spiritual paths. It would be better for you to listen to these talks over and over, even if they bore you. When you feel lost, remember not to touch anything outside. You know that the different spiritual modalities and paths are confusing you. So what is the point? Just let yourself be sober.

In your last connection you experienced much love, so trust that. That is what you love, and that is what you want to be in. Stay naked, stay empty, lose all these things, and see that you're still standing. It is simple. All this self-doubt and these fears are subsiding in you now. Just love it like it is. You have such lovely smallness in you; there is no need for self-doubt. Stand strong in you; you need to be you. Just be that strong, mellow, gentle you that you are.

Judgment of Self with Clarity

I'm in constant judgment of myself: good, bad, better, or worse. I really have a hard time accepting myself.

Take it one step at a time. When you are fully being in the clarity one step at a time, it will be much easier than putting many doors in front of you, not knowing which one to enter. You are afraid that if you enter one, you will miss what is in the others. You do know that you have *some* clarity; little by little, with tiny steps, be in that clarity and die in that clarity. Remember, take tiny steps. As you stand in that clarity, you are going to see your person, but don't *mind* seeing your person. It's way better than seeing multiple doors in front of you. When you have a little bit of clarity, stand in it kindly and gently without any expectations, with nowhere to go and nothing to achieve.

Then, as you keep seeing, include everything in that little bit of clarity. Everything depends on being in it. If you neglect this, then you will go back into the old self, and because you have experienced that wonderful clarity and now lost it, you will continue to suffer even more. You won't suffer because you *don't* know; you will suffer because of what you *do* know. You keep moving back and forth again and again. Be more responsible.

These questions come up all the time; am I learning anything, am I responsible? Accepting myself becomes more difficult.

You do not need to be okay. Accept that you are *not* okay. Value the part of the person you like the most, and don't fight with the person you don't like. You cannot win with the person you don't like. The more you think you'll do better, the more you will be defeated by it. You need to be standing with two feet in that little bit of clarity.

Okay, I see I am opening too many doors.

When you see multiple doors, you try to enter every door. That confuses you, and secretly you want to get through all of them quickly and not have to feel anything. Be in that clarity with nowhere to go, because it doesn't matter. See what that clarity does for you. You take care of that.

Clarity feels very important. Is it possible to be in this love and clarity on my own?

Fully being in it *now* matters. Fully allow that clarity as it is in your heart right now. You may not be excited at this moment, but you'll see later.

I am so grateful to you.

Let your heart look into the acceptance, and as you allow it to expand your heart, walk with it, talk with it, and sleep with it; do no more and no less than that. Now you know what all that softness is, so *be* in it all the time. You are already seeing the value of that tiny bit. This is what brings the wonderfulness. That tiny bit brings the smallness without any effort, without any mind understanding.

Yes. I see how the mind works; it's like it's all gone.

That is okay. It does not mean that everything is gone; it just means that now you know how to include everything in this tiny bit. Your tears are coming from that tiny bit of effortlessness, realness, and smallness. When you pay the cost, you will enter that space that is very inviting. But you can't enter and go all the way in without integrating all of you. The amount that is opening up is in your care now. When that part of you is opening up, it is deeply touching you. Stay aware of what it is like being that way. The amount that you are in doesn't matter; it doesn't have to be all of it. You'll see how strong that one touch is, and it is limitless. With one touch from that space (reality), there is no want or need. Simply drown in this one touch; just stay simple.

At this moment, there is nothing lacking.

Continue to move in this small touch of reality, and be in it without touching it and without worrying about the cost. That is the way. As you are touching it without doing anything but being in it, include the seeing. Be in the wonderfulness of being in both. You don't need to expect any results. Wonderfully be in it. If it lands somewhere, that's okay. If it doesn't land anywhere, that's perfectly fine. It's not your business.

Suddenly I feel tightness for no reason.

You are seeing more now. You can't neglect your person; include it. Include it by removing the labels without any reasoning. Include everything.

The tightness and aching are in my body, so include the body too?

You are forgetting to include your body. Whatever is happening in your body, include it. When you pay attention to only one part of you or you are interrupted by another part, you then neglect even more parts of you. That's why you need to be simple. Don't take yourself away from yourself. Be in the body just as you are with any feeling. You don't need to understand; you just need simple seeing and simple being, and you need to *be* in the body. When you don't pay attention to your body or neglect any pain in your body, then there will be a lack regarding anything you neglect or run away from. Continue including as you see, and instead of you entering a door, you will become a door. The more you include, the wider it becomes.

Shame and Embarrassment

I am completely scattered and unsettled in my life right now, and I am actually really embarrassed about it.

Through the embarrassment, enter you.

I'm trying to come back into me, but it's not working at all. I can't seem to find my center.

That's why shame and embarrassment work better than the trying. With that embarrassment, there is sadness. That is what you are trying to run away from. Don't run away from yourself; be in the embarrassment, and be in that sadness. (With awareness, be in these emotions, and don't try to make yourself feel better or make them go away.) Nothing needs to be fixed. Lay your head in them.

Is it just the running away? In the past you've mentioned my strong pattern of escaping into my thoughts.

You don't need to understand yourself. Whatever is happening, in the midst of that happening, you stay with what is more valuable to you, what is more collective in you. And you can simply trust laying your head in what is collective in you. As you lay your head in your embarrassment, you can't afford to sleep in it, and those unsettled feelings are helping you not to sleep. Don't bend in your weaknesses. Let yourself be awakened in your weaknesses. Instead of bending, stay in the kindness. Instead of covering or fixing, let yourself be softened. Use your opening to be awakened in it.

You told me that the unsettling is there to help me remain awake. That was very helpful, because I was trying to settle down.

In that trying to settle down, you cover up more. You cover up more of your weaknesses. Your weaknesses are being exposed in you, by you.

193

So stay naked in your weaknesses with the way they are being shown to you now. When you don't cover up any weaknesses and you stay aware of them, that will continue to let you see and to be more in that same naked way. Embrace your nakedness in a kind way, and learn to be comfortable in it. As you expand in this opening, and as you continue to be okay in this nakedness, this will let you be deepened in it also. Letting yourself be naked is the real smallness. You are tasting through the embarrassment. This breakthrough is wonderfully okay, and as you use it to stay awakened in it, let yourself be what it is bringing to you. This breaking through is removing the indirectness in you.

Right now there is so much embarrassment and sadness in front of me.

You are seeing, and you are trying to fix what you are seeing instead of staying honest in the beingness. This is the first taste of being awakened in your weaknesses, and it's not what you've been expecting from yourself. Instead of trying to settle down, love to be awakened in more of what is already opening up in you.

Is that done just by being in the embarrassment and sadness?

Yes. Be in the nakedness of what you are, stay in what you are, and let yourself feel what you are.

I can see how many wants and needs I have around my work project.

You are still beating yourself up. Instead of beating yourself up, kindly be in the nakedness of what you are. Expand in it and let yourself be, regardless of how you are feeling.

Are you telling me to be in my knowing?

Know the way you are feeling. You said you do feel embarrassed, so see more of what you are feeling about this. See what is being uncovered, and don't try to cover it in any way. It's simple. It's very much in front of you. Stay kind so that you can *be* that which is opening up in you.

I feel like I don't know anything.

Exactly. Let yourself *be*. That is real smallness. Now, through this opening, everything is out of control; before you were controlling everything. And through this opening, you know now how much you don't know. Through this opening, you know that what you've been controlling wasn't real at all. And that is what brings you back to the way you are feeling. That is your invitation to be in it.

I do feel a complete loss of control, and I feel I am not very smart.

You are just having a hard time accepting it, that's all. You do know that you never needed that control.

I'm seeing that much more now. What you say is very simple.

So you know. Allow the way you are feeling and where you are arriving right now to live in you. Don't just open up about your work; open up what you are. Let yourself feel without giving self-importance to the way you feel. That's how you let yourself expand. The self-importance in the feelings won't let you expand.

You mean I'm personalizing them?

Yes. This is the big awakening in you. Continue to remove the self-importance and let it live.

Could you please say more?

You are already beginning to like it. It's just that the liking part is still very little.

Am I feeling this only because I'm connecting with you?

You are aware through this connection that you *do* know how to be. Like it; like the way it's opening up in you. Even the taste is not what you ever expected. Begin to see what it is like to lose the control.

I do see that a lot is happening inside of me.

Yes. Expand in your happenings, and stay kind in your happenings.

How do you live in this all the time? I realize I'm used to living in such a small way.

And now you are living in a bigger way. Stay in the awe instead of questioning yourself. And as you stay in the awe, let yourself expand, and then learn to live without covers, little by little.

Something just happened here right now. It's like you pushed a button.

So is it good that you lost the control?

That's for sure. That control is limiting and tight.

You are returning back to where you can see; it's just a fresh beginning. It's much simpler, and in the being simple, it does feel like returning back to kindergarten. That is a wonderful place to start.

Yes, it is like a new start, and I will learn to take baby steps in this new start.

Yes, by embracing what you are, by being honest about what you are, and by letting your head rest in what you are.

Drama

I have never thought of myself as someone who creates drama. But I am beginning to see that I do create a lot of drama in my life. I come from a crazy family, and I am always allowing them to drag me into their battles. I seem to attract friends who have a lot of drama in their lives. I always thought that it was them, but now I realize that I have been a big part of the drama also!

And now, with this recognition and whatever it does to you, *like* being in it. Continue to give yourself to this brokenness. If you don't play at the surface with this, it will continue to take you deeper. If you fully sit in that part that creates drama, it will really open your eyes to how you have been living all of your life. It's not that you did not know this before; it's that the recognition was only intellectual. Now the inner real eyes are opening. They are only slightly open now, so keep widening them, regardless of what you see. This will show you the whole movie that you have created.

I would love to see that.

You just had a glimpse of it, so go back there; don't postpone anything. Go back the same way you did it just now. Differentiate what is real and what is not real.

Right now all I am feeling is such disbelief and shock, but I know I am the one who has created the drama.

Now you are in big shock.

But I love it.

Not fully; otherwise, there would be no shock. Now that you see that you are creating drama within yourself and your life, use this tiny bit of recognition to go into the wonderfulness of your seeing, rather than going into shock. See where the shock is coming from.

It's from me not seeing that I have lived like this my whole life. I always thought other people created drama, and not me.

So now you know that when you see something in other people, it's in you.

Yes, definitely.

Allow whatever feelings this recognition brings up in you. That is more important than the drama. Keep your head down. This seeing, if you are honestly in it, will bring the wonderful smallness within you. All the pain and all the shame will really wash you out if you fully allow it and stay in it all the time. It's in your care now. This seeing, even the little bit, is doing wonders for you. It's helping you to convert this pattern, but it is also shaking up your old self, which was causing you trouble. Wants and needs come in as soon as you try to change and fix yourself. Be alert so you can quickly see your hands trying to change or fix what you don't like. Do this quickly enough, and move with awareness before you get moved by it. It's not in your mind understanding. It is in where you never thought it would be.

So where is it?

It's in the tender shame. For you it's enough to be in that tender shame and remember tenderness first.

The only word coming to me is "gift." Such a beautiful gift you have given me.

The tender shame is the gift. The more value you give to this gift, the more you will see its wonder. You will see the beauty of this wonder continue in your life. Allow yourself to sink in the beauty of it. Then serve everything from that beauty, which has realness in it. This is much more effective than what you were doing in the past.

I'm seeing it more clearly now. My emotions were clouding my vision before.

The more comfortably you stand in it, the more you are able to see. You are seeing how your emotions are bringing in the cloudiness. This is a good start.

I really thank you.

Thank yourself first. Keep seeing that any tiny speck of cloudiness prevents you from being real. Always keep your mirror clean so you don't waste any more of your time.

Death and Grief

My life has fallen apart. My husband died suddenly this year, and I have been so busy taking care of the family that I haven't given myself space for my grief; I am afraid and overwhelmed. I keep myself from feeling vulnerable, and I am so depleted.

Be whatever you are instead of trying to convince yourself of what you are supposed to be. What you are feeling from this death is okay. You do not need to avoid this pain or be in service to others. It's okay; these are just doubts. You haven't discovered what is underneath this yet. Just come back into you; collect into yourself. If there is sorrow, there is nothing wrong with it; just do not participate in it too long, move through it in a direct way, and when you feel happy inside, respect that and move through that happiness.

Should I do that with the fear also?

The fear is not real; it's made up by you. You are so much more than anything that comes from your own thinking, your own believing. Even though you are familiar with your fear, it is not real, but if you participate in it and are bent by it, you *make* it real. See the fear as *only* a fear. See that clearly. Go inside to see what you are afraid of. See if you can lose this fear in you now. It is okay. Just lose it. You don't want to stay in that cloud and participate in it. The cloud is made by you. It's not real.

I don't understand. Are we talking about my emotions or what I am seeing as my reality? My reality is that my husband has died. Is that not real?

His death is real, and there is pain in you, but you don't need to throw yourself away in the pain. Don't dump (blindly immerse) yourself in the pain and give up. By dumping yourself into the pain, you are not opening your eyes in the pain. This death and that pain are actually helping you to wake up in you and for you. Now something is telling you to wake up in *you*. Death happens to everyone, so before you die, wake up. When you shed your body, you can shed it in an awakened way. Death pain is much more real than any other pain because there is no answer for why someone dies. This grief will keep taking you inward if you don't sleep in the pain. Use every opportunity to wake up in this.

My son tells me I seem distant.

You are distancing yourself when you close yourself off in that sorrow. Instead, open up inside you; but know that this will not happen overnight. Just slowly keep your eyes open in that pain; see it as a pain, and don't make something about it; just stay with it. Don't try to create an answer for yourself.

Will there be an answer one day?

Yes. If you diminish in your emotional body, it will be answered, but not in the way you are expecting right now. The more you wake up in everything, the more you will be facing the reality. Right now there is grief and worry, and the emotional body is inflamed. Everything has too much smoke. Don't *try* to find your way, but also don't throw yourself into that smoke as if that is everything. Stay awake in the pain and stay awake in your grieving body, recognizing that these are big emotions. See it as a grieving part (the pain), but don't go to the place of "poor me." Slowly you will become more comfortable in a direct way with that pain inside you. As you go inside in a direct way, then slowly your eyes will open more and more, and you will see more. The more you see, the more you won't throw yourself into it. It is just pain; it's a grieving part that you don't need to run away from, and you don't need to do something about it.

Just rest; you are not looking for any cure. If you are not changing it and not wishing to change it, then you will be *you* and a little bit more real than before. You don't need to be uncomfortable. Be comfortable and be clear; it is pain, it is the emotional body; be clear and direct in that; don't become one with it. If you let the grieving part take you over, you will then close your eyes, and you don't need to close your eyes. If you close your eyes from this pain, you will close your eyes from your *own* death pain. Your body is going to go. Use this now. Your husband's death is showing you how unreal you are living, and it is also showing you your own picture.

The shedding of this body comes, and if you close your eyes, everything is ugly, dark. Open your eyes while you are in the body, and face all unrealness inside you and let yourself *be in* the reality. Death then becomes beautiful, and you won't close your eyes against your own death. You will actually be waiting for it, and then when you go through any death, the grieving will be temporary and won't tear you apart. It's tearing you apart because you are not seeing that it is just pain. When you are sitting and crying, be more and more comfortable in it and say, "Okay, I'm crying and it is okay." Give lots of room inside you as you watch it, see it, and be in it.

So when I see it and be in it, are you speaking of detachment and watching it instead of rolling around in it?

Yes. Inside you there is dialogue, and you forget what is happening. But if you recognize what is happening in you, then you are not sleeping or throwing yourself into it. Learn to be awake in whatever is happening in you. That way you are standing in a clear way and you are able to give more room to everything instead of wishing it would go away. When you are not aware, you become very closed. Give lots and lots of room to the pain; it is okay. Expand in the pain so that you are not running away from the pain; then there will be nothing to feel bad about.

This is the *real* service to yourself. If you know how to be yourself, you will be helping your son too. He will learn that it is okay to be in his own sorrow. When you can see it and be in it, you're not closing; you're opening.

Being in this *real* service to yourself is a big responsibility within. Just keep going this way. Don't look back, and don't let the doubts come; just look forward in this. Some people cannot get out of the grieving part their whole life, but what is the worth in that? Use this opportunity. Pain helps a lot in waking up.

So pain is a gift.

Yes, if you use it with awareness to wake up. If you use it to tear yourself apart and roll around in it, becoming blind in the pain, then it's not a gift. This grief is helping to bring about more fire in you. It's really good.

Power

In a recent connection you said that I am using power in my life, but I actually think I am powerless. What did you mean?

Using power but thinking you are powerless is what it means to be self-important.

You said that self-importance is being powerful. So let's say that I feel I am not being recognized or acknowledged; do I then become even more powerful to get this recognition?

You are getting it now. Now that you know this, never let go of that little thread, because this is how you created your life and the negativity in it. First be comfortable in this. It may hurt you terribly, but this is going to be the turning point in your life.

At this point, why does it seem like I can't do anything right? Is that self-pity?

You had that self-pity before, and that's why I said to be comfortable in it. Now rewind to where you were. Do you want to live in this kind of pattern? Going back into the pattern is not going to be easy, and being in the pattern is not going to be easy. But there is freedom in doing that. Right now you are a slave to the pattern and you are blindly being driven by that pattern.

I go from self-pity to self-importance, and then I don't know how to stand up for myself. If I don't use that (power), where will I be? I realize I'm really unsure about the use of power.

Because you think you have no power, you create a negative power and a negative pattern—and for what? It is just for self-importance. You just said, "If I don't use that, where will I be?" So now you see that up to this point, you didn't want to be powerless.

I have it now.

When you say, "I have it now," be very comfortable in that and continue to see your discomfort. Be in it forever and ever. This is not a small pattern that you have. But the good news is, because it's a very big pattern, it will take you much deeper. It can take you deeply into you.

Why do I always feel that I want to make myself better?

Instead of being better, be real. Real is whatever you are now, no different from that. When you want to present untruth about yourself toward others by being different from what you actually are, then you are nicely covering your pattern and, at the same time, being driven by your pattern.

Control

Since my last connection with you, the desire to go within myself (to my interior) and trust myself is very strong now, and control in me is less than before.

You know, in every way, you need to give preference to your interior. The exterior is secondary. You have found the center you need, so now continue to diminish. Continue to be softened. This softening will continue to make more ground ready for you. The more your ground is ready, the more you will be able to diminish, and in the diminishing, you will continue to lose what you're holding on to.

When there is trust, making decisions comes from honesty of the heart. But when the mind makes decisions, it doesn't let you see the dishonesty. Give preference to the honesty within first, and use your honesty with everything in your life. By doing this, you will be able to integrate what you learn within. Give preference to your interior, and then as you are being in the exterior, remember—interior first. Dishonesty crawls in when you try to cover the interior and give preference to the exterior.

In giving preference to the interior, you will find over time that you do not want to leave it, and you will do everything to stay in it. When you feel that it is never enough, that will keep the fire alive in you. Enjoy seeing. See your control pattern and keep it in front of you, even though you don't like seeing this part of you. When you don't like what you see in you, you will secretly keep playing with it. So keep that control pattern in front of you. Be aware of it, and know when your hand wants to control. Stay in the kindness and embrace instead of trying to get rid of your control part and push it away.

Do you always have to stay with something you don't like, or will it disappear eventually?

Anything you don't like is there anyway; you just might not be aware of it. You only become aware through actions or reactions. Instead, just be in it. Being in the pattern lets you be awakened from inside.

If I keep the control pattern in front of me, will that stop me from controlling situations? This is hard to understand.

That's just closing your eyes to something you don't like, but it's only temporary. You are never free from whatever you close your eyes to. You've had a little glimpse of losing your control. You do know the taste of losing it, and you do like the result of losing the control pattern. So you are misunderstanding how to be in that pattern.

It's taken me forty years to learn how to control. I don't know how long it's going to take me to stop wanting to control my environment.

Be in the pattern honestly. The degree to which you are honest in your awareness determines how fast it will diminish. But don't look for results. When you look for results, you are actually neglecting being in the pattern. Even if it takes the rest of your life, be in the seeing of your pattern, because it's worth it. Learn to have a close relationship with the pattern by embracing the pattern in a kind and nonjudgmental way, because you don't want something that's a temporary fix.

That little feeling of no control has been wonderful. This brings more trust in me for this walk.

Then use that taste in everything. Nothing needs to go according to the way *you* want it to go. Love applying the softness and the kindness. Just love it.

Rage

Over these last few months, I have had lots of rage surfacing. That's not my image; my image is nice. It shatters me. I say to myself, "You are not nice, but everybody thinks you are; look how vicious you are." Is it good that I am seeing this side of me?

Yes, and that's why you are able to bring this up today.

It's a very dark side.

Dark yet real. This is how you are able to die when you are in the body. Swallow the sides you don't like; do so willingly, kindly, and gracefully.

I always wanted to be good. I thought I was being good, but now I suddenly see the rage in me.

It's only you discovering you. Recognize the judgments in you, toward yourself and toward others. This recognition does not mean that you should beat yourself up and say that you are not good. Just be happy that you are able to see this. Instead of participating in whatever is coming up from inside you, recognize it. You are seeing all the negativity that you have been feeling and have labeled; let it go back into your heart. When you take it back into your heart, embrace it as it is. Embrace all the pain as is and all the shame as is, and delicately be in it. That tender shame will do a lot for you. It will keep you in smallness, where you don't need self-importance. Self-pity is not required. When self-pity is not required, there is nothing to do. It's going to create a lot of discomfort in you. Now there is nothing to play with. There will be no story.

I wanted to be an author and write my life story. I realize that my story is completed today, and I don't want to write it now.

An ever-shattered ending.

I feel that I'm the sole player in the game of life and I played very badly.

And the beauty is that you recognize it.

You showed me.

It will be quite a journey to go back. Now you have a lot of responsibility, as you cannot neglect what has opened in you. Anytime you see it, or even when you don't see it, kindly invite it back, because as soon as you are unaware of it, it's going to play you again. Instead of letting that pattern play you, kindly and willingly be in it and just see it.

I was writing a book mostly about painful scenarios. I see now this would have eventually given me rewards and self-importance and allowed me to be in self-pity.

Even now you need to be careful not to participate in it. As soon as something comes up, be the first to quickly recognize it, and then you will be able to enjoy the death. There is no need for self-importance or self-pity; no book and no labels. Willingly let it happen in you. Once you totally die, everything is going to change. Doubts are still going to come, and being convinced by the doubts is still going to come. Just remember to be in it but not participate in it. The heart purity comes as you see the impurity in you. Kindly be in that impurity and let that impurity do whatever it does to you, whether it's tender shame or heartbreak. Just embrace everything as is.

Embracing everything that is impure is your forgiveness to yourself, but do not feel bad about it. Love being powerless by seeing how you are using power in your life, because when you use power in any way, it will always be harmful. It's never good for anyone to use power; whether it's negative or positive makes no difference. Be open so you can be kind, so you can embrace and be grateful that you can do this.

Impatience and Frustration

Yesterday I felt annoyance, frustration, and impatience because I got lost on the freeway, but I embraced this negativity and focused on my heart, and I felt happier and softer.

As you receive heart happiness, you don't need to satisfy yourself. Just go deeper—much deeper—where you will meet your roots. That is next for you, and that is calling you. You can't understand that which is calling with the mind, but you know how to follow it as you take that step. That step shows you how to trust, even when you don't understand. By being softened within, *like* going deeper. Use your frustration, anxiety, or whatever you can to see *you*. Use this to go deeper.

Gently invite all the feelings into you that you had when you were lost on the freeway. It doesn't matter if it is anxiety, anger, or impatience; invite it back into you in a friendly way. When you invite those feelings into you in a friendly way, you won't need to kill any part of you. Let yourself open up in those feelings, one by one. You don't need anything from them, not even heart happiness. You have already seen those things you don't like, so it is just a matter of inviting them back into you, one by one.

You believe you don't want those feelings or that they need to be different, but nothing needs to be different. Bring those feelings back into you in the way that everything is. Nothing needs to go the way you understand, the way you want, or the way you believe. Even if your old self does not like it, you don't need to change anything. Just let that door open where you see nonacceptance. When you don't change anything and actually allow everything to open up in you, then you know you don't need to show a different face to yourself. You can be the way you are.

Is this all an illusion?

Not until you actually can open up. You only perceive that it is illusion. When you perceive, you easily close that door by saying, "I don't need to go there; it's illusion." But that door is still there. Open that door and let yourself be seen by you; then you won't rely on your perceptions and you will allow yourself to be in your knowing. Perceptions can be based on beliefs. You believe that it is illusion, but you don't know *how* it is illusion until everything unfolds within you. Then you will know what illusion is and what illusion is not. What you saw is actually very real. It *is* in you, and it's been covered by you. If it's covered, remove the lid; and as you remove the lid of believing, there will be a lot for you to see. Allow yourself to be in the seeing in every way.

You look like a saint to me. I see a white halo that appears and disappears.

What does this mean to you?

I guess it means that you are special.

Whatever is special to you, take this to the deep in you. When you take this deeply into you, that will help you to go beyond every belief you have in you. You are able to move through clarity, where you just trust without including perceptions. You trust that little unfamiliarity in you. Allow your old self to diminish, regardless of how dear it is to you.

In my mind I see the world diminishing.

Don't make a separation. It is diminishing in every *way* that you are and *what* you are. Diminish in every way, and then you won't create any walls. You do know it is beginning now. In this diminishing, trust is your only support. It is not a good feeling, but just take those disheartened feelings in a dear way, as that is the only choice left. And you don't understand that choice.

It is time to jump.

I feel like I've jumped and I'm flying. It's beautiful!

You have a golden heart, so touch everything in the same way.

Pain and Fear of Losing

You always say, "Be with your pain." Recently I feel that when I am in pain about something, it feels different. I see the hurt, but then I don't see it. I can't seem to locate it. So am I just making the pain up?

Trying to understand your feelings and emotions as they change will confuse you. Even if the feelings about being hurt change, it's okay. Continue to choose to stay with it and go deeper in it, even if you don't feel the same way about the hurt.

You do understand this a little bit. In this understanding, just let yourself *be.* When you are wrapped up in mind understanding, even with the way you are being in the pain, you are losing the ground where you were letting yourself be in the pain. Just simply be *in* it and then let it change. It's okay. You are moving deeper, and that moving is unfolding more deeply in you. Even when your feelings change by being in the pain, don't pay attention to the feelings. This lets you move deeper and opens you up from inside.

When I am in pain and then it vanishes, I try to bring it back, but sometimes I can't find it again.

Because it's not about feeling the pain; it's about entering the pain. It's not something you feel continually. Being in the pain is just opening you up from inside, and as you open up, you lose the feelings about it. Feelings arise when you are tight and you are making too much of a fuss about it. *Entering* is opening you up from the inside.

So it happens by itself while I'm in this seeing?

Yes. Opening happens that way. Just keep on seeing it, and let it unfold *its* way—not your way, and not the way you're trying to understand this.

According to my understanding, because pain was not piercing me, I hoped that it meant it had dissolved.

That doesn't matter. Nothing needs to go away, including your pain; you just need to be in the pain. Being in it is opening you up from inside. When you are being in it, you're not being driven by it. You can just keep going deeper, as you have nothing to look upon behind or in front of you. Allow yourself to be in it. When you are participating in your emotions and feelings and being too personal with them, you will get hurt. Your expectations hurt you; wanting this to unfold your way hurts you.

Do I need to see my expectations and wants? When I say I don't see pain, am I just satisfying myself without going deeper to look at it? There is much more to see, isn't there?

Yes, much more to see. Stay open to seeing everything that you are by being aware of every thought and action and seeing everything that you are being driven by. Honest willingness and openness will help you to see. When you begin to recognize that you are satisfying yourself before going deeper, this will open the door for you to see more. It's only when you're just blindly satisfying yourself that you keep your door closed. It's much more than what you are open to right now. Remember this with every step you take.

I wonder why I am so afraid to stand strong in my truth and why I want everyone's acceptance.

If you have the key in your hand, you'd better use it regardless of what you lose. Take a little step of losing and bring everything you are afraid of losing in front of you. Love to lose from your side.

It's the fear of losing that is not letting me open. I know that it is me that is in my own way.

When you say you know, that knowing is valuable regardless of what you lose. When you don't stand in what you know, then you make big that which you're afraid of losing. When it's bigger than you, it blinds your knowing because you become too wrapped up in the fear of losing. Keep that knowing close to your heart, because you *do* know it is valuable, and now that you value it, make an effort to stand in it.

Are you saying I should stand in my knowing instead of trying to please everyone?

Yes. Then you will understand that you're not looking for truth outside of you. It's about turning inward. When you try to find truth outside of you, you easily justify yourself and identify yourself with others. This blinds you. When you value your knowing, that itself will comfort you. In the unfolding, there is nothing to hang on to outside or inside of you. You do know a bit, but you don't trust it. Trusting will shatter what you have believed in. Be more fire-full for the walk. Value your walk more than your life; this will help you to move fast. When you value the truth more than your life, then you don't look outside and you know there isn't anything worth saving. In every way, it is worth diminishing.

Fear and Anxiety

I realize that I have a lot of compulsive, habitual, addictive things I do (pills) to sedate or control my anxiety. I want to lose these protections, but I'm also afraid to give them up. I'm scared that the fear and anxiety would get so strong that I would die.

So is that basically your fear, a fear about dying?

Yes. Some of these deep anxieties stem from my mother dying when I was ten and growing up in the fundamentalist Christian system where they teach about burning in hell for eternity. This has created a lot of fear in me, and it is still there.

Yes, it's definitely there. Instead of returning into those thoughts and seeing those huge, scary pictures, stay with a small part of the picture— the very little bit at first—with kindness and gentleness. With the very little bit you can learn to *be* in it in a little way, and then you can return into the little girl within you.

Be little and be *in* the little. By being in the little, you learn to be very kind and gentle with yourself. With kindness and gentleness, nothing needs to be discarded no matter what you already have inside you. Just learn to be honest with the first step. Be very kind and very gentle with yourself.

And that baggage you have—any addiction, a lot of fear—doesn't matter at all. The more you protect yourself from these things, the more misery you create within you. Even though you hope you won't go into that misery, you are already sitting in it. You don't need to be afraid of what you call bad or miserable. You keep thinking you don't want to go into that misery as if it is somewhere else. That's why you need to be kind with yourself—so that you can be *in* wherever you are. The kindness and the gentleness are what will let you be in it.

215

Be kind—very kind—all the time, and stay closer to yourself by being in your heart. Be kind all the time, even if you have to remind yourself of this every single moment. It's worth it. There is no need to change anything at all; just apply kindness and gentleness to yourself. When you continue to apply the kindness and the gentleness to yourself, you don't have to feel good about it. It's okay whichever way you feel about it. Just know that you need to be very kind forever; then you don't need to run away from what you are already in.

I realize that I don't know how to be kind.

Even when you apply the kindness, don't worry about the dialogue. Just remind yourself you have no time for dialogue. Just *know* you need to be kind and gentle with yourself. You are already seeing everything in you; you just don't let yourself *be* in it in a kind way. You are already seeing that you need to be very kind and gentle.

You are very loving.

Learn to kiss your little hands, which are so busy trying to change and fix and clean. Learn to feel your face in a kind way. With the kindness, your walls are dropping. The kissing is reminding you that while in the kindness you need not work hard at all, because it is shedding naturally. Just be kind and love this so your heart can glow. When the kissing hands touch your face, everything will come back to life in you in every way. Kindness and gentleness are giving you new life.

I am afraid I don't have any kindness or gentleness toward myself.

In order to reach a place where you have the real kindness within you, first learn to apply the kindness from your side. Trust that you don't need to go anywhere, and trust that you don't need to go into a spiritual place. Just apply kindness and gentleness to yourself all the time with no judgment of self. This trust will bring you restfulness. Otherwise, having no trust will exhaust you.

The trust is so kind. This is so intimate; so tender.

You can trust that, and in the trust, where there is nowhere to go and nothing to fix, there is a little bit of clarity. Through that little bit of clarity, you know that you can touch more of you; and the more of you that softens, the more you come back to life. Then you won't hold back, you will cry happily in a very naked way. When you happily cry in a naked way, you're not grieving; you're touching your love. Grieving comes when you create the separateness, but in this, there is no separateness. You are including everything, little by little.

I'm hearing the words "Include all my internal junk and garbage too."

Kindness will happily include everything, and when you include, there is no panic and no anxiety. Including helps you to earn broadness. Now you know what this is and you know you have more aliveness. Touch and melt with trust, with love, with clarity, and with kindness and gentleness. That is how you *be* in it.

Unworthiness

I see that beneath almost every thought and action is a belief of "I am not enough." I was raised in a religious environment, believing that God expected me to feel unworthy.

Is that true?

No. At least the God part I know is not truth.

Exactly! Stay with that, because you know it's not true. When you stay with what you know *is* truth, then everything you're talking about will continue to shatter because you're not giving power to it anymore. You have been giving power to these habits of thought by making them big, and you have become buried underneath them. You have been trying to come out from under them, but your pattern of thinking is still giving them power.

How can I come out from under these habits?

You don't need any tools to come out; you don't need to use any effort to come out. (Effort means not accepting yourself with kindness and gentleness.) Instead embrace your habits with no judgment. You do know that what you are saying to yourself about "not enough" is not true; this is something you do know inside. Even when the distrust comes and tries to knock you down, know that this is not true. You don't need to feed anything; just stay positive with that little knowing within you. You are very hard on yourself and very negative about yourself. But it's okay; you don't need to change anything. You just need to stay with that little knowing, where you know that there is no truth in whatever you're thinking and saying to yourself. Everything is going to continue to bombard you, and it will get even stronger than before, but that doesn't matter. Stand firm in it by keeping your head down and knowing that you don't need to win anything—ever!

This little knowing is in *you* and not in your mind. Stay in that knowing within you.

I have a belief that seems to be set in concrete that says, "I have to try to change, or I will have lived for nothing."

But there is no truth in that; it is just your belief. Anything that is a belief, even if it is set in concrete or made with steel, contains no reality. Beliefs can take on the biggest forms, such as the belief in God, but they are still just beliefs. Don't be bent by your beliefs, or they will continue to come back into you bigger and stronger. Stay in the awareness, simply seeing, "Oh, that's another belief." Then what you are left with is softness.

I love softness; I like softness.

Don't let yourself be buried under your beliefs, which are buried underneath your thinking, thereby causing you to believe your thinking. Your thinking is buried underneath your negativity and underneath your hardness. Know there is no truth in that. Know that it seems to be true only because you are so used to being that way.

Be simple because being simple is valuable and being softened is valuable. By being softened, you're able to see much more, and then everything is okay to be seen by you. Then everything can continue to fall, which is okay. Know that what is falling needs to diminish in you, but don't touch anything. You know that all the beliefs and emotions will continue to come because you've been feeding them. What you have been feeding does not like to leave you easily, and you need not fight with them in any way; just stay honest. Stay honest and small and firm in what you know. From there you will know the deep. It is calling you. Then you will know even more than ever that there is no more time to waste at the surface. Live for what is calling you, because that calling serves a higher purpose. That purpose is not in your mind understanding; it is way beyond that understanding. Like this in every way in you from your side. Yes, it is possible, so kiss that possibility in you and adore that possibility in you. You can live for the possibility even though it's not in your mind understanding. It is okay; just trust.

219

What I'm experiencing right now—I used to feel this way a lot, but it scared me and I shut it down.

Now you can trust. Know what is true for you to be. Just continue to give to what is calling you, little by little. When you continue to give little by little, don't look back. There is no need to look back. You know your calling, and you know that there is only one way to go. Your readiness is there, and that is important; the rest of it will come little by little. Liking and loving this walk will help you to awaken to your true self. If you like and love this walk, your heart will also respond in the same way, and then you will be able to cuddle up in your heart like a little baby.

Addiction

I want to quit smoking. It's an addiction that I can observe building inside of me, and at times I lose my awareness and just participate in it. Smoking has a strong hold over me. I can see it's something I use to comfort and also to calm myself.

You don't need to fight with any kind of addiction. You don't need to fight with anything. The more you say, "Stop," the bigger it becomes. Just say to yourself, "I don't need to fight with this at all." Instead see your weakness and anchor yourself. Don't say to yourself, "I must go beyond this; I must get rid of this." Instead say to yourself, "I don't need to fight with it at all; I would rather see my weakness than fight with my weakness." You don't need to get rid of the weakness; just anchor yourself in it, because the problem is that you are not anchoring yourself in this addiction. You see it, you dip in, and you go out, over and over. If you don't anchor yourself in it, you won't go deeper.

You say to anchor in it. Does that mean stay with the discomfort of it?

Yes. Stay with the discomfort as it builds. Simply see it, and then stay in a small way, not fighting it. Just be in it a little bit; this is not something big you're doing. By *being* in the weakness and really letting yourself anchor in it, you will learn to say, "Okay, I'm going to go deeper in it." That will take you back into it and back into you. You have been getting frustrated because you have been dipping in and out, and now your person is getting trickier and is exhausting you. The addiction says, "You want to get rid of me? No!"

When you go deeper into your weakness with awareness, the weakness will then unfold. You are seeing your weakness more and more. You are hands-off and just being honest. The only thing you know is that you are going deeper; you know nothing else.

221

You don't need to get rid of that weakness at all. Going deep inside will give you recognition about the weakness (which is underneath the addiction.) Once you go into that weakness deeply and you see there is a block, that just means it needs to soften so that you can go deeper into the weakness. There is no need to look back. Even if choking comes and you feel you can't breathe anymore, just say to yourself, "It is okay; it is not a big deal." Decide to simply go into the weakness with no returning back. Then you will begin to understand by going down into the deep. More and more heart understanding will keep coming as you move into the deep. Allow it, but at the same time, do not do anything. Do not even expect anything. Don't ask yourself, "Do I still want to smoke or not?" You don't have time to look, whether you do want to or you don't want to.

You *are* becoming more responsible now. And it is a very beautiful thing to go deeper. But this doesn't mean there is no discomfort. As you go down and down and down, you leave your mind behind. You can go very deep in this; you can do so because you *are* able to. Your mind will probably say, "No! You can't." But look at this falseness first; look at this addiction first. Just fully trust in one thing—fully trust in *you*. Even if sadness is crawling in, don't budge. It is okay if it comes in; just keep going deeper.

Even if it doesn't feel right, that doesn't matter; it doesn't need to feel right. Familiarity always feels right, but it's not right. It's tricky. That sense of not feeling right doesn't matter; it can rest. Just say to yourself, "It is okay? I need to go deeper."

It is like stepping into an elevator and just allowing it to go down to the bottom floor.

Keep allowing it, endlessly. Even if it scares you and all the floors are gone and you don't know where you are going, just trust. It is okay. Even if there is a black hole, just keep going.

Okay, I can feel fear and panic.

Yes, this is okay; just trust and move through that fear and panic. You are able to go into the deep blackness that is just like a cloud, and you are still able to move through it. You have become much softer already. Keep going; keep going. There is no reason to stop, right?

There is absolutely no reason to stop.

So slowly learn to stay in the deep in you in every way. When you learn to stay in the deep, you are much more grounded, much more connected, and not so up-and-down at the surface. When you are connected, you are then able to see shallowness in everything. You are going to see the shallowness more and more, and everything will drop, and you won't need to do anything. Your work is to stay in the deep.

It feels a little like some experiences I've had with drugs, but this is not scary. This is way more real and feels safe.

Anything besides this reality won't let you keep your eyes open. Music, drugs, addictions—your eyes are not open with these things. In *this* way you are sober and your eyes are open. As long as your eyes are not open, this is only an experience, and it stays as an experience, but then you become thirsty again. Even though you will come back to the surface, and even though you may get lost many times in the beginning, you still know you need to go back into the deep. Now you are beginning to know how to go there.

It's like falling.

You need no mind understanding in the deep. Don't try to force it; understanding comes by itself. You don't even need to look for it. The more you fall, the more you are in the deep. The clouds are slowly leaving, and you will begin to see the way you are unclear with yourself. You will recognize it. Just allow with no trying.

The shallowness is jumpy, up and down, and the deep is like the ocean; the deeper the water, the more still it is. Stay in the stillness, and then you will see that nothing harms you. What you were worrying about before now seems so unreal. Anything that was bothering you about your addiction, see that it is just your weakness that you keep repeating. Take it to the deep, and stay with it until it really unfolds in you. When you learn to open your eyes in your weaknesses, then you don't use anything to close your eyes. Any addiction is about trying to put ointment on something; it is a way to close your eyes. That is how everything drops as you earn the heart knowledge.

It seems as if I spend a lot of time being afraid of the sad, fearful, angry places inside of me.

Visit those dark and angry places. Choose to visit them, and then they are not big. It is only when you choose *not* to visit them that they become big. Keep walking forward, and go very deep. Don't just open the door and barely touch them and then run from discomfort. That creates too much up-and-down at the surface. Everything will show you what you are holding on to inside of you. You may say that you know, but when you say that you know what is in there, your mind will then trick you. Instead let it unfold in you. You will see that the real knowing is when it unfolds. It is very subtle.

My mind is like a crazy monkey.

When you stay in the deep, you are not feeding that part of you at the surface that thinks this is crazy. You think you have to find some way to stay calm at the surface so you can cope. You have been trying to manage yourself. Stay in the deep and go very deep. Now you know the dark cloud, the fear, cannot stop you. Nothing can stop you. *You* choose.

Disappointments

In my life there have been so many disappointments that I can't get back up on my feet; I am beaten down by life right now.

The disappointments are directing you to your inner self. Anything that you think is working out in your life is also a disappointment to your real self. Instead of trying to fix your life, let it take you to your inner self. As you allow it to take you to your inner self, it will soften you. With softening, you will be able to enter within.

When you try to fix things outside of yourself, you go even more into the outer world, and the more outer you go, the harder you become. Instead of complicating matters by trying to fix things in your life according to what you think is right, simplify them and don't make a big deal about them. Make things simple, and that simplicity will bring you back into your heart. Reconnect with your heart instead of getting tangled up in your mind with fixing things. Everything seems disappointing because you long for something different. Be kind with yourself first in the midst of all the disappointments. Continue to be in the kindness, and then there will be no room for fixing, expecting, or protecting. If you try to ignore what is bothering you, you actually tangle yourself in it even more.

Be simple. Allow yourself to be simple. Now you are not trying to fix. When you are not trying to fix, then you will have a little more clarity to let all things be the way they are with a warm heart. If you don't embrace with a warm heart, then you secretly will make everything complicated. Have warm okayness with all your disappointments. In the warm okayness, you don't expect anything and your wants and needs can rest in your heart.

As you let your wants and needs rest in your heart, regardless of the situation, you enter within, where you know it's true to be. In that little bit, you can grow by being warmly okay in every way. Warm acceptance is the real beginning, which has no end. In the warm acceptance, you don't avoid the pain; you just warmly let the pain enter your heart. The warm acceptance of the pain is able to crack the shell around your heart.

Hope and Expectations

When my partner and I decided to be in a close relationship and move in together, I saw how much I feel restricted in my freedom when I am in a relationship.

Don't analyze these things as they come up in you; instead, step into them. When you step in, see what comes up in you; that will show you the root in you. Keep your door open so you can be dearly in anything that comes up.

I can see the tendency for my mind to look for solutions; it wants to modify situations, and it spins around in my head.

Your responsibility is to dearly be in whatever comes up to the surface. That does not mean that whatever comes up will necessarily be seen all the time. But stay in the sharpness, and as soon as you see the face of what comes up, dearly embrace that face and be in that face forever. By embracing and being in that face, you will be able to expand, and the space that you are living in will also expand. Then the room is not going be too small or too tight for you. You are experiencing tightness because you are not embracing that face, and being in that face is not a good feeling. But let yourself be in that feeling wonderfully without hoping that the feeling will ever change.

I can see that hope is still there, because I know from experience that feelings are changeable like the weather. A good example is hoping for good weather when there is bad.

Hoping for good weather won't let you expand. When there is no hope for good weather, the discomfort comes, along with disappointment. That's why you need to stay honest. When any little hope is alive in you, then you still have the back door open. As long as the back door is open, you release yourself from the pain of your discomfort. Stepping into the discomfort helps you to expand. As you are expanding within, your mind may still give you a hard time, but don't believe that. Stay in what is true for you to be. Hopelessness is a dear friend. Choose to dearly be in it.

When I am in hopelessness, it doesn't matter; the weather doesn't matter.

Including and seeing what is *not* true can be difficult. Even if it is difficult, you can be gentle. When you are very gentle with the difficulty, it becomes a little softer, a little easier to stay in.

I have had a lot of difficult times, and I have repeated the same old story over and over.

Even if that story is being repeated, it's just asking you to include, because now you are able to include.

Suddenly the old pain that was hidden pops up now, and I can include it. Sometimes I am amazed by what comes up when I am in your presence!

These surprises are good news to your real healing.

I trust what you said, and this trust always brings me back from the mind stories.

Because in this trust you know the surface doesn't matter, but the surface is doing wonders within you.

Is the surface helping?

Yes. This is because you are letting trust in; you are choosing to stay honest, and you are okay with what it is costing you.

It's like only a temporary disturbance and nothing more.

Yes! This letting in removes the walls, and then you can become more than you have ever been. Your earnings are still there; you just had a little turbulence. After the turbulence you will have even more clarity than before.

Acceptance Does the Unlocking

I realize how stressed I am in my life. I am even stressed because I feel I'm not good enough for your teachings. This pattern is part of my whole life; I feel this way with everything all of the time.

There is no need to carry this stress any longer. Patterns are bad only when you allow them to run your life; then they create blindness and suffering. The more you give them power, the more you feel powerless. You give them power even when you know you're suffering from them. It takes time to be in your patterns so that they don't drive you, but they still help you.

How do they help me?

When you see those patterns one by one, you are able to take yourself closer to the real self. Accepting your patterns without changing anything will help to take you deeper—deeper than the self that you are familiar with now.

I just realized that I don't have much trust, and right now something is changing inside of me without me doing anything.

What were you doing until now?

I have always tried to find solutions in my mind, but I realize now that it doesn't work and nothing changes.

As soon as you realized that it doesn't work, that very honest seeing opened up a door for you.

By "honest," do you mean acceptance?

Acceptance does the unlocking for you and gives you a new door for you to enter. Accept your entrance and continue to accept within and without you, regardless of what it looks like. You will begin to see beauty in everything and to see wonderfulness in everything. As you continue to enter, it will move you through the whole wonderland.

It's very important for me to try to go deeper even if it's very difficult.

It is the other way around. Acceptance is taking you deeper and deeper without trying. So when you want to go deeper, your hands may want to come out again. No hands equal a magical world. Just continue with acceptance. Praise the untrue part in you.

I have lots of trust now and not a lot of protection. Thank you so much. I know you are truth, and I love you for that.

When you speak, speak from the smallness and only with what you know is truth. Practice being less in everything, even in the use of words. Words keep you away from realness.

Physical Pain

The pain I have been carrying in my heart is reflected in my body. It's hard for me to find that place where I can have complete acceptance of my body. There is a lot of discomfort and pain. I want to be softer and be accepting of who I am without conflict.

That conflict is created by you. When you don't accept the way you are and try to be the way you *like*, that doesn't solve any problems. It doesn't serve any purpose other than actually adding more misery. This misery is felt because you don't know how to lay your head down in the way you *are* and with the way your body *is*.

Give up trying to fix yourself. When you try to fix yourself, you will only make everything worse in you and outside of you. Trying is not going to work. Little by little, learn how to lay your head down. That is the reality. You think you don't want to face it, because it is easy to believe in the doings instead of facing the reality. Begin to face the reality. It's a complete U-turn from your doings. As a person you don't like this, but in the deeper self you just know how true it is. Respond to what is true for you to be. Anchor yourself in that little bit of reality, and let the rest of it fall down step-by-step. Trying to get rid of that part that feels misery is not the honest way, and being in that little bit of honesty will shake that part.

When I move into that place of honesty, I feel compassion for myself, and I can embrace myself more from that place.

Little by little. Never think about the cost. Just love moving forward.

It feels like starting from scratch in that place of vulnerability and rawness. That's old stuff, and I don't want to look back anymore.

Exactly. When you turn within, don't look back at the outside world. When you begin, it will be like being a baby. You have to learn to take steps to see and be everything that is inside you. But always remember that these steps are not for you to grab; you are taking steps because it is true for you to be. When you take the steps because it is true for you to be, then whenever the doubt comes, you are able to take the support. Learn to stand with the honesty instead of with what feels right and wrong. What feels right and wrong always confuses you and keeps you in the shallow. Always do this in such a kind way. That's how, little by little, you will come down from your perceptions, from your mental ideas. The trust comes little by little as you keep moving through your distrust. In this joining, learn to give your whole heart. As you like your softness, just lay your head in it with a sweet welcome to a clean heart.

Change of Health

Thank you for helping me with my health. For the last twenty-five years I have suffered. My health has improved a great deal, and I do not cough anymore.

Your emotions are changing.

It is because of your grace.

As your interior is changing, your exterior is changing too. It is you. It is not so much about healing, but it happens as *you* heal. Move cleanly and simply.

You give much love.

That is because you are able to allow that love inside you. As you allow the love, you will then become love. Everywhere you look, let it be in everything, and as you open yourself up, you'll see the whole universe is love. The more you open, the more the amount of responsibility will increase. As you embrace the responsibility, you will grow more and more.

I had none of this until you came into my life. You changed my life.

You did.

Stay Kind

I am always fighting in my mind, and it is hard for me to be kind to myself.

The whole heart, all of it, is why you are here. Long to die in this. Make it easy for yourself. When you're blind and trying to understand, simply come down where there is no understanding, and the trust will then grow. Stay kind, because there is no need for fighting, no need to fight the mind. Stay kind even to the mind—very kind. When you are kind to your mind and to yourself, you will slowly become able to see why you were being so hard on yourself.

When you are being hard on yourself and trying to change yourself, you are not able to see the kind of self you are. You don't need to expect anything from yourself; just continue to apply the kindness and the gentleness all of the time. It doesn't matter what you see in you; just allow. It's okay. As you stay kind, you stay in the nakedness.

I am trying to identify the flaws that I have, and when I see them, I want them to go away.

No. That is feeding the unkindness. When you feed your wants and needs, you may feel good, but that has nothing to do with kindness. Feeling good is always temporary.

Then what am I looking to feel?

You don't have to change your feelings; you have to *recognize* your feelings. Kindness occurs when you see that you are being hard on yourself and when you are protecting yourself. Even though you don't understand kindness, you don't need to waste your time trying to understand it. Just come back into you and *be*.

Because you have mentioned it multiple times, I feel I should understand what being kind to myself means. I am still struggling with that.

Being whatever you are will show you where you are unkind. When you are able to see the unkindness, then you will know you can be kind. Trying won't let you *be*. In trying, there is always loudness. So instead of participating in the loudness, just come back into you and be in the okayness. There is nothing to change; nothing to fix. Only see and be and embrace everything you are.

Happiness

You said that wanting is dishonest. I am very passionate about my career. Is that dishonesty, because I want it and I am very happy with it?

Being happy with what you are doing is okay as long as you are not satisfied with that kind of happiness. When you are not satisfied with that kind of happiness, you will always have a window open, and from that window there is a possibility to open up even more. If you don't have a window open, sooner or later you will find out that what you call happiness is not real happiness. At the surface, everything is temporary. It doesn't matter how you feel, how happy you are about something, or how deeply passionate you are about something, because it's not permanent.

Earlier you said that all the fun and excitement is lost when you achieve this bliss. How do I convince myself that I want to awaken if this is the case? This world is so tangible, although I know it is not permanent.

Let the secret come out, and bring it in front of you. When you see this secret about what you call happiness, you will then see that it is not permanent and that it is temporary.

How do I live in this world after awakening?

You live in the world in a much better way. You won't live with the unrealness; you won't live with the shallowness. What you call happiness, as you know it, is shallow. That happiness is carrying wants and needs, and you only *think* you are living. See the shallowness. When you face the shallowness, it will actually break your heart. You just said, "How I do I live in this world after awakening?" That in itself shows you that you have fear because you think you will not be able to live. That is a lack of trust. You don't trust yourself. Just trust. Whatever is on the surface is there today and will be gone tomorrow. That is reality.

This reality knows how to live openly and fearlessly. Don't live to maintain that temporary happiness; live for what is permanent in you.

Right now, being with you, I feel some kind of change in me.

A moment ago, you let in what I was saying. That is valuable. You don't understand that letting in, but that letting in will transform you completely. Because of this little movement, you are not going to be the same anymore. What you let in will sprout one day when you choose to live for it.

What you let in needs your heart's water, not your mind understanding. As you let it in, don't deny what you are letting in. This way you will always nurture it with your heart's water and it will grow. This growing has nothing to do with happiness and unhappiness. This growing is beyond everything you are familiar with. Being in this little shift in you will show you even more shallowness at the surface. The more you recognize the shallowness at the surface, the more your grip at the surface will be loosened; the more you are okay with losing the grip, the more it will let you land in the deepest in you.

Nakedness

Earlier you said, "Let yourself sink." What did you mean?

Your ship is able to sink when nothing at the surface is your business anymore.

So are you saying that the well-being of my family and loved ones is no longer my business?

Yes. Your ship won't sink otherwise. Being in that powerlessness lets you be comfortable in your nakedness. You have a habit of going to a space that is a protection for you. Instead of *being,* you go back into your mind, and when you go back into your mind, there is a space where you see things in a more powerful way. But when you are being in the nakedness, you don't see those things, because it's very simple in the nothingness. Just differentiate between both and admire your nakedness more than anything else.

Nakedness is the simplicity?

Nakedness is nothingness, and in that nothingness you easily feel everything instead of making up beliefs about things. Nakedness is feeling, seeing, and being. Value that in your heart, and learn to live that way. Being in the rawness, in the nothingness, all the time will give you birth.

When I was a little boy, I had to get stitches, and I felt embarrassed because I was so afraid. With this nakedness, there is deep shame about being afraid.

Yes, and isn't that beautiful? Learn to be comfortable in that shame. In that tender shame, continue dying; you have been longing for this.

Very badly have I been longing for that. I see my nakedness. It's not that I see my body. I see rawness; I see everything exposed.

Yes, and from that everything is now entering the direct way. Learn to live from *that* space instead of from your mind. Learn to be comfortable in your nakedness. That way you will feel more.

I can see the cover that I have put on so that I don't have to feel.

And in that nakedness, you don't need anyone with you. When you feel comfortable in your nakedness, then any part of the person you are carrying within you will drop. That will bring even more aloneness in you.

It's like a lifetime of being afraid of this.

Because of that fear, you are not able to enjoy the beauty you have already earned.

I feel very ashamed to have virtually used my entire life this way. I have been driven to cover everything up.

Now comfortably allow your shame to be naked. It is okay in this nakedness. It's earned by you and for you; it's new. It is time now for you to embrace that little boy who was afraid of getting stitches. Embrace him without any reason, without any expectations. Open your heart to embrace him, and embrace your nakedness and the little boy's innocence.

I will embrace him.

You can be together now.

I feel as though I want to apologize to all the people I ever met for using them for my purpose.

Nakedness allows everything, and in the nakedness, you don't need to lift your hand or your head for apologies. Just let everything come back into you, because you are ready. When you are naked, your head is down and you are completely and very comfortably open. Let everything come back into you from every direction.

I know what that means, but I don't understand what that means. When my head is down, I am looking at my nakedness, my rawness.

Just be in the nakedness. You can trust that. Bring more simplicity into your heart, as nothing needs to be done.

When you said, "Let everything come back into you," it just started flying back!

As everything returns into you, just remember to keep your head down. And even if you don't understand what is happening now or for the rest of your life, it is okay. This little boy doesn't need anything.

I pushed him away for so long; I covered him up. I am embracing that little boy.

Embrace with an open heart without sympathy, because the boy doesn't need any sympathy; he needs your heart. Open your heart for the little boy as is. The boy doesn't need anything. Pick out all of your stitches fearlessly.

I want to break all my stitches and just let my heart expand, and I want to know that I am my heart and there is no separation. It's all heart.

Yes, keep opening; you are able to break all your stitches now. Slowly the little boy will learn to speak. The little boy can be in the awe forever because of what the little boy is seeing. This is the future for you.

I love the beauty you are. There are no words.

Now you know that this dying is worth it. This dying makes it possible in every way.

I very much want to die to be awakened.

This is a big responsibility. Learn by being as is, and in this, learn to trust your innocence. Innocence doesn't cover or protect.

Oneness

What is oneness? Is experiencing oneness a step of this learning?

As you learn with each step, whichever step you are in, you can be one with that step. Each step you move through takes you to the emptiness. From the first step, it is the same. When you are one with that emptiness, then total acceptance takes you to that oneness that is not in any way imagined.

If you are focusing on understanding oneness, you'll miss where you are at in that moment. Just *be* in your own step fully. Any bigger understanding than that does not serve any purpose. The tiniest little step serves a big purpose. As the questions come, don't touch them; just learn to keep your head down. As you go step-by-step, not touching the questions in the mind, the questions will shatter as you allow shattering.

Everything that a person carries is baggage. Openly be with the baggage to see what you are carrying. When you recognize that it's not worth carrying and it doesn't feel good, then it's worth being in oneness. Every idea and belief keeps the person in narrowness, and then the person never enjoys the freedom. Everybody likes freedom, but nobody likes the feeling of letting go. Like letting go more than you like your feelings. This will remove your suffering.

Being in Bliss

Almost daily over the last few months, I have been in bliss, if you want to call it that. Now and then the old self will pop up with patterns, but I can recognize it, and I'll go back and stay in the bliss.

Yes, you are in the bliss, but as you enjoy this bliss, keep giving preference to your patterns. You prefer to be in the bliss more than you prefer to be in your patterns. Even in that bliss, stay sober by not giving in to your preference; otherwise, you will easily grab on to the bliss. Anything you grab on to, especially pure bliss, will be hard let go. Stay in it as it is, and keep moving forward. It is always like that; as you earn, you will receive some rewards. Each time a reward is given, enjoy it and stay in it, but don't hold on to that reward. Broadness of the heart occurs when you keep letting go of all the rewards and keep moving forward. You can stay in it as long as you want, but it's going to end up the same; it's not going to satisfy you. Your heart is opening, and the bliss can land in it.

This is very sobering, if you want to call it that. It's like I'm drunk in the day with this bliss. Right now I feel it, but I am sobering.

You are sobering because you are allowing the bliss to go back into your heart. Your heart is opening to that drunkenness in a simple form. In order for you to be in the absolute, you have to let go of everything. It doesn't matter how good, how big, or how tasty it is. That form is earned by you gracefully; always include your person in this.

It feels as if there is a door and I can open the door and I am home. It feels right.

Know what you are neglecting, and know that what you are looking for is more satisfaction. Don't set the goal, but do include your person. Home is not that. In moving toward home, you lose everything—even the desire to be home and the belief that there is a home. You may not like that, but that is the truth. Everywhere you land, you think you've finally landed. But after a while you're not going to be satisfied. Your heart is still going to break more in this journey. Willingly go into your dislikes both ways. Go deeper and deeper inside of you, where you totally lose what you were thinking and believing.

I can feel my heart breaking now. It's taking me to a much greater depth, and I am dropping deeper and deeper into the bliss. I am going into the unknown.

Completely drown in the unknown, where you totally lose your identity. Continue to include your person in this drowning. Hold no preferences. You have capacity, and your capacities are unlimited. And *never* satisfy yourself in anything.

Entering the Deep

I was so excited to go to India and travel with my boyfriend, but now I have no excitement about traveling anymore. I just want to keep walking in this journey.

What you know within is not small in you, and because it is not small, you cannot deny that at all. Dearly embrace this shift, and as you dearly embrace the shift in you, don't hold back the grieving of your past. Simply let it move through you. Keep trusting; keep moving.

It's the biggest shift I have had, and it makes me trust you more openheartedly than ever before, and all I want to do now is be with you and keep moving forward.

What you have lost is that dark part of you, and what you are in now is wonderful brightness. Adore this brightness; live for this brightness so you can diminish for this brightness in you.

I was always wanting and needing. I feel like I don't need anything anymore. I am content with this walk and moving forward with the "new me," and it is so clear now. I couldn't see it before. It's my new truth.

Forever stay in your heart, and by staying in your heart, stay powerless and be humble. By staying in your heart, you will slowly learn to enter the depth of your heart. From there you can see you have a great deal of depth in you. Because you have that much depth in you, nothing else will satisfy you. The depth has been earned by you, and now you know your readiness for this walk. This readiness can scare you a little bit, but just keep trusting. This being scared is obvious because your mind doesn't understand any of this. Even if there is disappointment from your whole self, just let yourself expand from it, and that will also help you to be in it more than before.

The loss of my old self is so worth the gain.

Your deep is wide open; that is your calling. Respond to your calling by losing what you are hanging on to. You do know how to do this. In this responding there is disappointment. If you keep hugging your disappointments with such a tender heart, that will let you be in the deep. It has been decided by you, and that lets you be what you are and what you want.

Awakening to the Real Self

In this connection, an individual is guided by Gurpreet to the awakened state.

I had a dream that I was looking out the window and I turned away. I still see hardness inside me. I know that softness is the way to be. If I am in softness, I let it live; and being in hardness, I bring "my way" in it.

Don't turn your face away from anything. Face everything as it is. That itself will help you to soften and stay in the deepest in you. When you are being in the deepest, you just don't live here and there. You are more grounded in the simplicity.

My discomfort comes in, and then I see that it is me who is making something big out of it.

Yes. Making something out of it doesn't let you stay in the deepest in you. Being in the deep forever will help you to diminish by seeing everything as it appears in front of you.

Right now I keep seeing more trust, and I am learning to trust my feet totally.

Yes, the more you trust, the more you allow yourself to be in the deep in you. Be in the deep regardless of what appears or how big it appears. Love that stillness where you allow everything to diminish in *its* way (higher self). When you let everything diminish *its* way, you won't turn your face away from anything. Face everything.

Yes, face everything as is. I am beginning to see that this is how I become grounded in that. It's like I am aware of my old patterns. There is something here for me to invite in. I have been keeping it separate.

You are forming something where you now know that you don't need to keep it separate.

246

I gave it form a long time ago, and it is there.

Value trusting your own feet. Make anything you see simple. It is only when you don't trust your own feet that you make things hard or extraordinary, including your learning. When you create something extraordinary, even if you turn your face from it, it will still be in your way. Anything you create that is extraordinary, trust your feet and be in that stillness. Allow this so it can diminish back into you.

So my experience lately is something I created?

When you make a big deal, you are just seeing a different face of it. You are being softened; it is simple. What appears does disappear.

So it does disappear when I am softened?

As you trust your feet and when you are not in the way, the child grows in a simple way.

I am making a connection with another dream. A child was kidnapped and blindfolded, and I found the child and took the blindfold off. So now I see I blind myself when I am in the way.

You already know how to trust your feet. When you know how to trust your feet, then, in the trust, keep your head in your heart.

I see. When I trust my feet, I will be walking with knowing and not understanding.

Yes. What is that like to you?

I feel so touched by this knowing.

In the touch, just be with the simplicity of your heart.

Now I am making another connection with the way I am choking myself.

When you get touched by what is so dear to you, just stay still, because your splashing closes your eyes.

The splashing is not allowing it to land, and this is where I am making it mine. I have a taste right now of walking with knowing, and I love that.

Walk in a simple way. When you walk in such a simple way, you will let that child in you live and grow. Even if you have choked yourself, just remember to stay in it, and simply dive deeper into your choking. In the diving deeper, remember to open your eyes until you let yourself unfold in it. When you unfold yourself, you will know you don't need to come back to the surface. You are going deeper and staying deeper in your choking, which will actually broaden you. In being broadened, you earn more trust, and then you can do it in a much simpler and easier way.

I see the simple and easy way. It is like the understanding is slowly disappearing and I just trust the knowing. It's so simple. I see now. When there is no trust, I come back up.

In this trust, everything softens and begins to disappear.

I am just recognizing the excitement in what you just said, and I do see that. It is as though I would like to be awakened in this pattern.

You do choke yourself, so enter it and then stay in the deep. Stay in the deep and continue to go even deeper in it. That will clean your core beginning where the pattern started from. Each pattern keeps walking with you. Remember, you need to enter the pattern, and when you enter, absolutely give everything to stay in the deepest until it really unfolds in you. Those patterns are helping you to go deeper.

I am more aware now. I looked at those patterns as weaknesses, but now I see that they are my companion to help me stay in the deep. I can feel it melting. (The heart is softening.)

There are no compartments; you are able to melt freely. That longing appears because of you opening up. Just be in it.

A part of me sees that this is where I need to stay continuously, but then another part comes in wanting to choke.

Simply see, but do not touch; then the choking can come and disappear.

I am recognizing that on one side I love this and on the other side the choking is coming in, and they are both walking side by side. I see that I continue in this and that I must remember, like you said, not to turn my face away.

Do not panic. Be the way you are now; that is the taste.

I see that the smoothness is there, and I see what is not there, and I see that I am to include it. It is very smooth.

In this smoothness everything is changing very fast.

It is like I am recognizing that I have to have my hands off. The controlling part wants to come in. I have to be willingly loose.

In this willingness, you are already losing even your name.

I had another dream. I gave my ID to a girl to photocopy it, but my face on the paper came out choppy and I could hardly recognize my face.

Yes, as you have no old face.

Now I see this is how I live and walk in knowing. I am not able to understand this, but there is a clarity that this is the simple way.

This is the simple way, the dear way, and the real way.

Yes, and without choking. In this there is only oneness. I see there is no ending.

This is the beginning.

It is so nothing! I have been making something out of this, and it has walked with me to this "no ending." I remember talking to you in another meeting, but it was as if I were not there.

Knowing was there.

What I see is that I am being replaced by knowing. I see that the "old" is there and wants to do its job. In embracing it, I feel that it wants to come along.

As your face changes, the old will learn your new ways, and as you live from this, everything will come along from the old self and will also be replaced by this "new way"; this is already beginning to happen.

I am aware that the old is lingering around. It is as if it is not in me, but outside of me.

You know that you are able to open up to anything as long as you don't make it a big deal. Know also that the wall is diminishing in you.

I see the old habits, and it will take time. The old is still functioning and wants to keep its label. I can't give any name to this.

You are learning to live where there is no name. Continue to make this happen through the trust.

The trust is helping me to ground. Something is coming up, and I keep holding back. I see my discomfort. I see trust, and I need to trust.

This is because you are standing on unfamiliar ground. Your trust will help you to stay there. With the willingness, you learn to live in it.

I see the willingness to stay in it and the willingness to lose; there is no grabbing.

Even if the discomfort comes, being in the new ground is okay. If the distrust comes, it is okay. Even through the discomfort and the distrust, you can still see. Through the seeing you are able to trust more of what you already know.

Now I see the testing ground.

As your walls are diminishing, along with anything you see of the old self, you are able to see through. Seeing through is like you are seeing your dishonesty, and at the same time you know.

I know not to touch it.

And love letting yourself land in every way.

This is helping me to diminish more. I feel very grateful for your guidance. It is very easy to go astray.

Little by little. A little trust is an invitation for more; a little bit of knowing is invitation for more.

I keep seeing a finger pointing to the little bit, indicating that I should keep this really close to my heart. I see it is saying to trust honesty, and through honesty I am able to come this far. Without honesty all I was doing was saving myself. But saving myself for what? It doesn't make sense.

Yes. Now it doesn't, but before, it did.

I see excitement is about to come, and I say, "What for?" All the familiar things—there is no meaning in any of those things. All my life I have been giving value to all the wrong things. And now I see the value was hidden, and now I can walk with that value.

Yes, that is why I keep seeing your name spelled in an opposite way now: Radha.

I see that so much is here, and yet not so much. I see that it doesn't make sense, but it does make sense. It is as if I am seeing both. It is as though they both exist together. I want to touch your feet, but I see that your feet and my feet are the same. I am in awe, and I will stay with this, and I thank you so much. Just trust; just trust.

Pure Awareness

In this connection, Gurpreet guides an awakened individual to diminish and go deeper into pure awareness.

I recognize the importance of being in discomfort. It brings me into my feet. Yesterday I didn't know where I was inwardly, but as soon as I remembered to be in the discomfort, it brought me back. When the music started today, I let the music move through me.

In the discomfort, you are seeing it in the way it is. It is not something big, not something that shouldn't be there. The discomfort is there, and that's the way you are alive; just see the discomfort as is and see that there is nothing in it for you.

I see it opens me up more, and I don't feel it as much, because there is more room now. I see the habit of making something out of it.

Don't give so much room for self-judgment. You self-judge when you say, "I don't know where I was; I was moving through the music." As long as you simply have the awareness, then it is okay. It is okay and it is no big deal. This is showing you, even more, how to *be* in it. This is showing you how to *be* in discomfort and not make anything big, because it's not big at all.

Yes, it was just an automatic reaction, and now I am more aware.

So you see, even as you are saying this, it is expanding.

Okay. More awareness. Be in the trust, and be in awareness. It is free to do whatever it wants to do.

Exactly. When you believe, "It is mine; it is doing something to me, so I have to keep it," then you start owning it, and as soon as you think you own something, the suffering starts. This applies to everything. So see everything as simple play. And seeing it as just play, you will move through everything freely. Only when it is not play do you then lose your awareness in it, and then you feel pain.

Now you are expanding more and more, and what is there? Only pure awareness. That awareness is earned by you because you have seen a lot of you over time.

Oh, now I see; it boils down to not feeling anything. It's a big nothing. That's what I went through for a few days before I came here; I had a glimpse of this freedom, and then I recognized that there was a panic about that freedom, and in that panic I started to create.

Yes, and what you just went through right now was that you felt panic and started to create again.

Once I start to create out of panic, I see busyness growing, and the world is there. But why couldn't I see that freedom?

It's just a denying of freedom, but freedom is there. Even at this level of awareness, you are in the person and you are still able to create.

I was going to act on it, but I realized that I couldn't continue to be a slave to my thoughts. In this freedom it is like the world is not there. That's when the panic came, because I left the world behind.

Yes, exactly, because there have been many times when I have tried to take you there, but you panic.

Yes, and I didn't understand why I felt panic.

Now slowly walk there yourself. I know the way you are; you're going to walk there slowly, little by little. There, now you are walking. It is so simple.

I see where I am now. The shock was brought about because the world was totally behind me. It seemed so scary, and I don't know why, but I wanted to go back to the familiar.

Even though you have naturally found yourself in this awareness, if I told you right now, "Go in there," your panic would return. You would say, "No! How can I go in there? I don't know what's going to happen." This has been with you from the very beginning. When you panic, everything is gone; you lose yourself, but it's just panic, that's all. Now you are naturally seeing this, and you say, "Oh, this is just awareness, that's all. Empty." Through this you're able to recognize this world and that it *is* behind you.

Yes, I want to clarify. In the creation, I was able to go to that world and do what I do, but in that there is also a freedom. Oh! I see there is a freedom either way.

Yes, that is what I say; this whole world is okay, and everything in it is okay. It's just that now you have that awareness where you recognize the whole world *is* okay.

I also had a glimpse that on one side is nothingness and on the other side is the world in which there is everything, and in between is where I live. Therefore I am free from both sides.

You were standing in the middle and trying to decide which way you would go. Before this, you were in the world, and that's why panic came first. You were thinking, "I'm leaving the world behind and I'm going there to nothingness." It felt like panic. But now you are clear and can see both sides, and that is awareness. Being in the awareness unfolds everything about the world. Everything is okay; it was just the "me" who wasn't okay. It was the "me" who was participating in it blindly.

So I can still go out into the world, but with awareness?

It is really that you *are* awareness. You don't *go* with awareness, you *are* awareness now. Awareness has no form; it's nothing. Now there is no world, but just simple awareness. You have the recognition now about the world and that the world is just a play. If the world is just a play, then you are awareness.

My head was in the future. It was saying, "What am I going to do next?" But awareness is only the now.

There is no future, because the future is the mind and the past is the mind. This is awareness. You cannot get anything from it because there is no storm, no bad weather, no forecasting, no gain, and no loss.

A part of me that is still insecure wants to know a future. The insecure part is still alive from the person and wants to know. But already I am aware of it.

In you, everything can come in a playful way now. Previously, everything was in a panicked way; now it is in a playful way. Awareness doesn't mind if there is nothing.

I see a new playfulness in me. I am learning how to walk with that.

It's hard to believe you are in the awareness, isn't it?

Yes.

Even as the play starts, the awareness does too. Every part of you wants to be recognized in the awareness. Everything is okay. That recognition is important. Allow that to move through also.

I'm looking to feel it, but I won't feel it, because I am awareness.

Awareness doesn't mind that nothing is happening; what is happening is just in the person. Every wave is coming, and you're aware that you now know that a wave is just a wave and has nothing to do with you. Now there is a lot of space for the wave.

Another way to put it is that this is a new learning and you don't know how to *be* in it yet. A part of you is still looking and questioning. This is just another step for you to learn how to *be* that awareness, and that you will learn for the rest of your life. Don't get lost in what you have earned, because some people who have earned the awareness do get lost. You do understand what I am talking about.

Now learn to be just *you*—*pure* awareness without a person. No person—not even a little girl or boy, no going up or down. You *are* awareness now, and you are recognizing it, and if you don't stay in your own recognition, you will be hanging on to forms. Now you see the unrealness of the other world—that dream world where things come and go. They are meaningless.

I am being in this awareness, and my mind keeps searching for things and cannot find anything.

You see that awareness *is* you. The mind is just familiarity. See with clear eyes, sober eyes; this is just mind, so it can slowly vanish in your heart.

I was going to say I must focus on the heart, but there is no focusing on the heart either. No focus is necessary.

No focusing, nothing. You *are* awareness now. That is the space you now have in you.

What I see right now is that slowly my mind will come to rest. It's still operating a bit. I now see my mind slowly coming to rest, and I am more in the body.

Even in this coming back into the body, you're still awareness. You're just not hanging up there now; that's all.

As I am in the body, I can feel the expansion. I remember, more trust. I am not doing anything, and it is just happening.

Yes, it is happening.

I keep seeing the word "universe."

You are. In this "now" you are merging into the universe. Your mind is not there, and you are pure awareness. It is simple, nothing big.

It's nothing. I cannot describe it.

That's very good. You have earned this much awareness, this much honesty, and that is letting you be one with it. You can go into it more and more.

I see that understanding is not here. I cannot understand. This is totally different from understanding.

This is new to you. It's not as if you will stay like this all the time. You are learning and earning more and more, but now in a more impersonal way, an awareness way.

When you say impersonal, I see that I don't need to understand anything.

Yes (laughs). And that is the trust.

When you say trust, it reminds me to give all of me to this.

Now you taste that first taste of awareness; that itself is inviting you. How can you not give all of you to this?

I feel touched by what you just said. It takes me into devotion; I call it devotion.

Yes.

My whole life I haven't known devotion; everything was for me. Now it is not for me.

This devotion and this love keep you plugged into the awareness. Your eyes look on this. This is the love forever . . . forever. When your eyes are in this love, don't look back. Just live for your love as awareness.

When I look back, I see no one needs me. The family doesn't need me. When I look back, I see it was me not knowing what to do with myself. It wasn't about them. I remember it wouldn't let me go back. It wouldn't let me.

This devotion won't let you. This devotion is for the awareness.

I see that in this moment of looking back and wanting to turn back, it wouldn't let me, and at the same time I was happy to keep going on this walk. It works in its own mysterious way. I was not planning to be here in this particular retreat, but here I am, and look what is!

Nothing comes in your way, because you *are* in the love.

I see the full picture now. It will help me keep my face in one direction, and if any surprises come, that is okay. What's so clear to me now is that I thought my family needed me, but they don't need me. That is so freeing.

When your direction is honestly toward the higher self, everything is being taken care of. Everything! Everything is being taken care of in *its* way, not your way. That is what the trust is about. Keep your face in the trust. Everything is working *its* way, not your way.

So now you know who was making you panic. (Gently laughs.)

I choked myself. I couldn't breathe. I didn't understand why there was all the panic. (Laughs.) How many ways can I say thank you to you?

You entering is a thank-you.

The Taste of Sweet Death

In this connection, Gurpreet guides an awakened individual to diminish more and to go deeper within the awakened state.

I am beginning to see that I should just give up everything and simply let go and trust that.

So you see a part that is itching in you because the person wants something. But it is not getting anything, and so now what is coming up is that big bubble of distrust. You don't need to participate in it. You don't need to lose yourself in it just because you are not getting what you want.

I don't know what to want or where to go.

But the habit is there. The mind always wants something, and when you become smaller, it's like you are not getting; you are losing, and then what comes up is the distrust. So even if the biggest bubble of distrust comes, just stay still as you watch. The mind is so used to saying, "I want something; I want a little bit of understanding." Now you are beginning to trust, even though the mind is not getting it.

The distrust was very strong this time and lasted for a few days, but then it dropped.

Yes, that is natural, and that is what I'm saying. When you begin to trust, even when the biggest bubble of distrust comes, you wonder, "Where am I going?"

Yes, I was wondering, but I was much more settled after that distrust. When you were talking about longing earlier, I felt there was so much pain that I wanted to run, because nothing is satisfying. I have become very sensitive, and tears keep coming; I can't stop them.

It is okay. Stay still; you don't need to stop anything. Everything will stop by itself; just continue to lose every comfort.

Right now I don't know what to lose. Can you help me see? I know I don't need anything.

You just mentioned that you don't need anything. So if you don't need anything, then just drop. The dropping is not like falling back to sleep; that is giving up. Just stay awake. What you are giving up is your own personality, your own expectations, and your own distrust. So let it happen; you don't need to stop the process. You do not need to carry anything. You feel like you need to carry your holdings in order to be awakened. Now let yourself lose in the awareness.

I see that losing is easy when I am able to see my holdings.

That means that you are still holding on to something, but if you are not holding on to anything, then there is nothing to give up. You mentioned that you feel like giving up. Then give up! Let yourself see what happens.

Just now I was able to see that I was holding. I am going to try to give up right now.

Give up! It's like you know something is heavy and you are tired, and then your frustration comes in and you want to run away, but it's just the mind playing tricks with you. It's the mind creating the disturbances that shake things up and make everything unclear.

I am feeling a lot more softness and quietness, and I am realizing that I don't need to hold any of that; it can just go.

Okay. Keep going; nothing is needed; just keep going.

I can drop everything, even the knowing, and then there will be nothing needed. I see this is the biggest trap—to hold on to anything in order to move into nothingness.

Yes, you need nothing, absolutely nothing.

Yes. No love, no joy; nothing.

Nothing, nothing at all.

I can drop myself into needing nothing.

And this continues, being in the *nothing needed*. Even if distrust comes, just say, "I don't need you either." You need nothing.

Yes, whatever comes up, I can just let go.

Yes. Everything can go. Absolutely everything can go.

Tiny wants and expectations come up so easily.

It is like the more you go down, the more will come up. You are just seeing it, and it can join where you are going. You don't need to join what is bubbling up; just let what is bubbling up join in you as you are resting.

When you said "resting," I felt there is a rest, but still there is a kind of restlessness there also.

So that's also a bubble. It's like you are sitting beside water that has been there for a long time. There are tiny bubbles on the water, and you are touching them, and as you touch them they make noise because you are disturbing them. But continuously stay in the rest and just be aware of every noise that is coming up: your wants, needs, distrust—anything at all. It may feel so dry, so nothing, so dull, but that is okay. Just decide to rest. You may say, "Okay, I'm even losing my longing." I say to you, lose your longing; you don't need anything.

Right now, because of the longing I have, the losing is happening.

Yes, so you are just *using* the longing, that is all.

I'm using my longing to drop, and that's okay.

And as soon as you don't need that longing, it too can go.

That brought the sadness.

Yes, and even complete darkness. That's okay; you don't need that either.

Thank you. I'm even letting my longing go now. This is bringing about so much sadness in me.

Be in the sadness, but you don't need to give any importance to what is happening *from* the sadness. When you give importance, you say, "I am sad," and that means you are giving importance to yourself. The sadness itself is not causing you trouble. Saying "I am sad" is where you are being big. You are able to give up your joy and your love, and yet why are you holding on to your sadness? Everything can come and fall on your plate. It's okay; embrace it all. If you are still choosing, that means the person is still alive in you.

Thank you for making that clear; now much more can go.

Yes, that is going to show you more, and don't give importance to what you are receiving.

Actually, it was very good when you said something about giving importance to the sadness. I see how easy it is to give importance to even longing, and I hadn't seen it that way until now.

You see the "I" is behind your longing, and because of that there is much attachment around the big "I."

Yes, everything can go simply now.

And when *simply* everything can go, there is no wish. That is a complete surrender. No expectations. It's like, if I'm letting everything go, there must be something that needs to happen.

The beautiful part is that even the receiving can go. I don't need to worry about anything.

Everything needs to go, and not for now only, but forever.

Yes, it's very easy to give importance to even a little bit of receiving and then hang on to it. To have no importance for this nothingness is necessary; otherwise, this nothingness can be something. It's so beautiful. Nothing is needed, nothing at all.

Yes, that's very nice that you can see that also.

Thank you for showing me this; I never knew! Even the delightful way. All can go; there is no more sadness in it.

You are taking the bitter pill the sweeter way. It is not bitter anymore for you. This is the beauty, and it's so fast.

I'm seeing so much dearness everywhere, and it can all go too. This is fun that everybody and everything can just go. I just saw that even you can go!

Yes, absolutely everything needs to go; absolutely nothing needs to stay.

You are making it so simple, so easy.

There is a flow in which you are seeing what is happening, and you are in the beingness in what is happening.

I just saw everything go through my feet, and I am simply being. My feet are very warm, and I am just being with this warmth. There is fun in all of this, but this fun can go now too.

Yes. Everything.

Yes. Even as I am recognizing this, I realize my recognition can also go.

That's how the seeing keeps coming effortlessly and the losing happens effortlessly, and it just keeps coming.

Now I am not in my body.

Yes, so now you know you are *not* the body.

I'm nothing. The feeling of no ground was there before, but now I am in no ground.

You need no ground now. When you are not the body and when you are not the mind, everything is much more alive.

Yes, I am feeling that there is no sadness or anything at all. Everything just vanished. It's only this left now.

Yes, so you know now that you are not that sadness and you are not that anxiety or that distrust.

Yes, there is no fear, nothing. How do you do this to me?

You are the one who is doing it.

You are the one taking me there.

Now this nothingness can move through anything.

I was experiencing no body and just awareness before this connection, but this is very different. It is so wonderful to see that every little thing can go: the happiness, grace—everything. Nothing is required in this. It is so easy to let go in this.

Yes, you are in *huge* permission to where every part of you is just opening up. Your mind is not yours anymore.

Your feet are so dear to me, and even that is going, and the devotion can simply go also. These tears are so different.

They are impersonal tears.

In this the words "I love you" come, but even that I can't say.

Your big "I" is also impersonal.

More of the same things are continuously dropping, such as more love, more joy.

This is because your mind is opening up and experiencing everything.

This distrust that "it can't be me" just came up.

That also can go.

Yes, it is so beautiful. Every little thing can go. I need nothing and no amazement.

Yes, and yet it is amazing. This amazement is so impersonal, so rich.

Right now it just felt like my heart opened up so differently, and now I know where everything is going. My head is completely down, and being this small is something I have never known before.

Yes, this is the beginning of this meeting. You are meeting you.

It's like my arms just opened up, and I want to give my real self a big hug.

You are.

It's like I don't know anything about it and it's just that I am simply being. I am entering this little bit as it is happening now.

You are entering in a big way.

From here I can see that experiences are not important at all. Letting them go is more important. Every little recognition and acknowledgment can go. It is better that everything goes. I just saw how wrong I was in all of this in a really big way.

Yes. This is the simple way.

It seems so easy right now because the complications of the mind have dropped.

So *who* was the trouble?

Me! I see all around me in a huge way how wrong all of those unnecessary perceptions and beliefs were.

So no more death for you.

Last week I was experiencing that I was cold like a dead body. It felt like the coldness of death.

Now you are being in the warmth of the death.

Yes, I do feel the warmth. It's simply lovely, but this lovely has to go too. This is how nothing stays. Everything is so much brighter now.

Being impersonal is seeing and being.

From here everything seems like new; I am even seeing you as new.

Yes, only when you warmly die. This is the taste of sweet death.

It doesn't feel like death. There is now so much more aliveness, but a different kind of aliveness. It is almost like nothingness is the only thing left; none of the old self exists anymore. Only what is "now" is left.

When you stay in the beingness with this endless letting go, you then won't give birth to the "I" again, even though you are still in the body.

Every little bit is coming and dropping away. So that's why there is no more creation! It is fun; tiny happenings are coming and going as a flow. It's simply fun to be that way.

Yes. One is flying through everything.

In this awareness the tiny mind comes up, but it quickly drops away. I don't even know how to thank you in this.

You enjoy this in an impersonal way.

Forever with you. Forever.

Acknowledgments

Thank you, Karen Six, Kiran Mitra, and Uma Seths, for the countless hours spent transcribing the sessions in this book from audio to paper. Thank you, Amandeep, for your technical assistance. Thank you to my husband, John, for his invaluable support.

Carole Davis-McMechan

Glossary

A

arrow—One's attention
awakened—A state in which one has come to recognize ignorance
      and the created self
awareness—Conscious wakefulness

B

be in it—To be aware while in a pattern, feeling, or emotion
be in the feet—To be humble and surrender in a loving and respectful
      way
bending—Giving in to your weaknesses
beyond—Letting go of familiar ways and moving toward the true way
      of being
bigness—Mind-driven self-importance
broaden—To expand

C

clarity—Clearheadedness; doubtlessness; sureness and solidity
cover—To hide one's unreal and dishonest ways from oneself
created self—The surface identity that we perceive we are

D

dearness—Preciousness
deep—The space that is not on the surface
diminish—To die in and move beyond
direct way—The way without mind dialogue or story

discomfort—Uneasiness one experiences upon seeing one's
      unacceptable behavior

dishonesty—A lack of truthfulness with oneself

doer-ship—The position of one who fixes and changes things to one's
      own liking

drunkenness—A condition of being under the influence of a state of
      mind and not recognizing the real picture

E-F

embrace—Total acceptance of what opens up in you

face—Your attention

face away—To avoid seeing something; to be in denial

face toward—To see everything about yourself even though you don't
      like it

fire-full—A state of giving the highest priority Longing is felt
      intensely in this state.)

flying—Not staying humble or grounded when one experiences
      happiness and excitement in one's life or goodness in oneself

form—Anything that is tangible within you

formlessness—That which is progressively beyond all that is familiar
      and unfamiliar to you

free fall—A state of letting oneself move forward without using any
      support

from your side—In such a way that one is willingly making an effort,
      even though one feels one lacks this ability

G

grounded—Humble, not flying

guest—A disliked habit or pattern that is seen by us (If we treat these
      items as guests, we will easily be able to embrace them.)

H

hands—Any beliefs, ideas, feelings, or even earnings used for the gain of our created self

head down—Humble; not making a big deal regarding your happenings, and surrendering to what is

heart—The real you

heart-full way—The unlimited way, which is open to everything

holdings—Things you are afraid to let go of

honesty—The quality of being true to yourself regardless of the outcome

honest way—The way of taking things in without judgment

I-K

impersonal—Not identifying with the created self; taking things in without any judgment

irresponsibility—An unconscious way of being; a way of blaming others or situations

knowing—Undisputed understanding from deep within

L

land—To comfortably step into what you are presently experiencing

leaning—Not standing straight

lessness—Smallness, diminishing

little bit—A segment of whatever one is in that can be dealt with without trying to tackle everything at once

M-N-O

nakedness—Comfortably exposing oneself in one's weakness

nothingness—A state of being where nothing can be touched, felt, or seen; a place where nothing exists

ointment—Something that provides pain relief

P

park—To satisfy oneself in a certain space or stop oneself from
    moving forward

participate in—To identify with anything

patterns—Any automatic behaviors developed to protect one's created
    self

person—The created self/ego.

purity—Pristine cleanness without self-interest

R-S

real self—Who one really is (also called the higher self or true self)

reality—That which is beyond the person; the true/real reality

responsible—Conscious about everything within you

satisfy yourself—To go into comfort, park, and/or not take
    responsibility

self-realized—The condition of knowing one is awakened

sinking—Free-falling with trust

small—In lessness

smallness—Humbleness

sober—Not excited and clearheaded

stand straight—To not need anything at all; to have no leaning

surface—Daily life in the world constructed by the created self
    (family, career, money, etc.)

T-U-V-W

threatening the person/ego—Engaging in unannounced war against
    the created self

touching—Interfering and naming

weakness—The systems developed in us to protect our "I"

About the Author

Gurpreet's words grace these pages. The simplicity, the wisdom, the truth, and the love that this book conveys come directly from Gurpreet. Carole Davis-McMechan compiled and edited Gurpreet's rich material that comprises this work with the assistance of many volunteers.

Gurpreet is an awakened teacher who emanates unconditional love and total acceptance to everyone who comes to see her and be in her presence. She is an embodiment of truth and simplicity and is now taking her teachings out into the world in the form of a book.

People who have been thirsty for the truth have found it in Gurpreet's teachings. Many of us, as we have received her wisdom, have felt a great need for her teachings to become a living book for all to benefit from, and so this book came to be.

Gurpreet is currently holding retreats across Canada and many other countries around the world. To find out more about Gurpreet and her retreats, please visit her website at www.awakeningwithgurpreet.com.